# Praise for
# *Widowed Walk*

Amid the pain and grief from the loss of a spouse, we look up and ask, "Where is God?" The words "you need to know you are not alone in this" is what separates this book from so many. Pastor and Author Gary Roe has once again solidified his status as the "go-to" resource for people struggling with grief. Keen insight and practical approach are how Gary Roe consistently and compassionately touches on the subjects that widowed spouses going through grief actually need to hear, like "It's ok to grieve". *Widowed Walk* takes it to the next level by combining his knowledge as a top grief counselor in with his heart of a Pastor. A must read for spouses going through the pain of grief.

—Scott Willmore, Senior Pastor,
The Word Community Church

"Grief is a daily journey after the loss of a beloved spouse. Gary Roe has captured the essence of this struggle and provided on-point encouragement for each day of the journey. Well done!"

—Dr. Tony Taylor, Senior Pastor,
Hilltop Lakes Chapel

"A widowed griever's journey can be painful, lonely and overwhelming. *Widowed Walk* filters our feelings with faith, reminding us—we are not alone. God walks with us every step of the way."

—Dr. Charles W. Page, MD,
author of *A Spoonful of Courage*

"Gary has done it again! *Widowed Walk* hits on all the emotions I have heard widowed spouses speak about during my time as a Chaplain and leading support groups. I believe that all who read this book will be able to relate to the emotions and find comfort, affirmation, and hope. The way faith is incorporated with the grief journey is refreshing. I have not found material that speaks about the challenges of prayer, scripture reading, and church attendance during the grief journey as *Widowed Walk* does. I will be using this book for future support groups as I know this is going to help spouses break through barriers and into spiritual freedom."

—Jessica D. Wilson,
Hospice Chaplain, Life Coach

"The grief journey is unique to every widowed spouse. Those who are Christians have a God that knows this personally. Jesus, when He walked around among us, experienced grief. He wept. In *Widowed Walk: Experiencing God After the Loss of a Spouse*, Gary Roe uses God's word to create daily readings where the griever walks with God. The tough questions and emotions are addressed head-on, allowing the reader to experience the Jesus, the Balm of Gilead, to make them whole again."

—Glen Lord, Board President,
The Compassionate Friends,
President and CEO, The Grief Toolbox

"Gary offers real, raw, and rational discussion on grief after the loss of a spouse. He brings the practicality of experience and the truth of the Bible to help soothe the suffering soul. Grief is a journey, and Gary leads the reader from hurt to healing."

—Dr. Troy Allen, Pastor,
First Baptist Church College Station

"*Widowed Walk* is a collection of comforting blankets to wrap around your shoulders when you are feeling the pain of the spouse you dearly loved. The words speak directly to your grieving heart, reassuring you that you are not alone. The short chapters make it easy to pick up and read for just a few moments at a time."

—Kathy Trim, Missionary Care
and MK Care, TEAM Japan

# WIDOWED WALK

EXPERIENCING GOD
AFTER THE LOSS
OF A SPOUSE

# GARY ROE

Thank you for purchasing
*Widowed Walk: Experiencing God
After the Loss of a Spouse.*

These pages are designed to be a companion
for you in your grief journey.

Please don't read this book just once.

Pick it up again in six months or a year.

Come to it again and again.

Each time you will be at a different place.

You'll see your progress. You'll be encouraged.

And you'll find your hope has grown.


As a thanks, please accept this gift – an exclusive,
free, printable PDF for readers of this book.


Download yours today:

**Scripture and Prayers from *Widowed Walk***

**www.garyroe.com/grief-prayers**

# Other Books By Gary Roe

**The God and Grief Series:**

*Grief Walk: Experiencing God After the Loss of a Loved One*

**The Comfort Series:**

*Comfort for Grieving Hearts: Hope and Encouragement in Times of Loss*

*Comfort for the Grieving Spouse's Heart: Hope and Healing After Losing Your Partner*

*Comfort for the Grieving Parent's Heart: Hope and Healing After Losing Your Child*

*Comfort for the Grieving Adult Child's Heart: Hope and Healing After Losing Your Parent*

**The Good Grief Series:**

*Aftermath: Picking Up the Pieces After a Suicide*

*Teen Grief: Caring for the Grieving Teenage Heart*

*Shattered: Surviving the Loss of a Child*

*Please Be Patient, I'm Grieving: How to Care for and Support the Grieving Heart*

*Heartbroken: Healing from the Loss of a Spouse*

*Surviving the Holidays Without You: Navigating Grief During Special Seasons*

**The Difference Maker Series:**

*Difference Maker: Overcoming Adversity and Turning Pain into Purpose, Every Day* (Teen Edition; Adult Edition)

*Living on the Edge: How to Fight and Win the Battle for Your Mind and Heart* (Teen Edition; Adult Edition)

*Saying Goodbye: Facing the Loss of a Loved One* (co-author)

*Not Quite Healed: 40 Truths for Male Survivors of Childhood Sexual Abuse* (co-author)

# Welcome
# What This Book
# is All About

**"It's okay. You're strong. You'll get through this."**

Chances are you've heard something like this. It might indeed be true, but it's not particularly helpful.

When we lose someone we love, especially a beloved spouse, the people around us don't know what to say. They end up saying what they've heard others say. They mean well, but clichés and platitudes do little for a grieving spouse's heart.

You need something more than this—far more.

You need to know that it's okay to hurt, to be sad, and to grieve.

You need to know that you're not crazy and that your grief is "normal."

You need to know that you're not alone in this.

You need to know that you will get through this, even though you will not be the same person you were before.

And most of all, you need the comfort of God's presence. You need to experience His compassion and love. You need to know He is walking with you in your pain and grief.

And that's what this book is all about.

## THE LOSS OF A SPOUSE IS PAINFUL.

The loss of a spouse, a life partner, is painful and crushing. It breaks our hearts and shakes our souls.

Amid our pain and grief, we look up. We wonder, "Where is God? Did this have to happen? Why?"

Loss invaded my life early. Sexual abuse, bullying, disappointments, failures, deaths, estrangements, and divorce riddled my childhood. I grew up feeling damaged, sad, and lonely. I was functionally orphaned by the time I was 15. I wondered if I was going to make it.

I said to myself, "If this is what life is like, I must find a way to handle the hits that come. Then, I must find a way to use the pain for good, or else what is this all for?"

In my simple teenage way, I prayed, "God, only you can do this. If you don't, I'm history."

I've been on a journey of healing ever since.

## OUR LOSSES PILE UP OVER TIME.

I wish I could say I've experienced less loss and pain since my teen years, but that is not the case. The losses kept coming. Some of them were deep and even debilitating. Over time, they piled up and threatened to crush my heart. Even in my darkest moments, God was there, embracing me in my pain and whispering to my wounded heart.

He kept me alive. He has led me through the valley of the shadow of death many times. He continues to bring healing to my injured soul, though never quite in the way I ask for or anticipate. And, true to His loving nature, He continues to take my losses and use them for good, in my life and in the lives of those around me.

God has certainly answered my simple teenage prayer. My adult life has been about helping hurting, wounded people (like me) heal and grow. Over the last three decades as a missionary, pastor, and hospice chaplain, I've had the honor of walking with tens of thousands of souls through the valley of grief. Dealing with loss, death, and grief has become my routine.

I now spend my days writing, speaking, and counseling. My focus is simple: meeting grieving hearts where they are and walking with them there. As we do that together, I believe God speaks, comforts, and brings healing.

God meets us in our pain and embraces us. He journeys with us through the emotional upheaval, mental confusion, physical distress, spiritual questioning, and relational changes. Jesus has personally experienced more pain, suffering, and grief than we can fathom. He knows. He gets it. He is the best grief companion imaginable.

God walks with us in our grief. That's what this book is about.

*Widowed Walk* is essentially a grief devotional, designed to be read one chapter a day. Take your time. Open your heart. Be honest about your thoughts and emotions. Allow Jesus to meet you in each day's reading.

And remember...

It's okay to hurt.

It's okay to be sad and to grieve.

Though the loss of a spouse can be devastating, you will get through this - but you will not be the same.

You are not alone. Far from it. God is with you in your pain and grief.

God loves you where you are, as you are. If you're willing, He will bring healing and growth to your broken heart.

He will somehow use this terrible loss for good in your life and in the lives of those you touch.

I'm honored to be with you on this sacred journey. Breathe deeply. Take your time. Read on...

# 1

*How did this happen?*
*My love was just here. How can this be?*
*My heart is stunned. I'm in shock – immobilized.*
*I stare at the ground in disbelief.*
*What am I going to do?*
*Lord, help me.*

———◆———

Stunned. Shocked. Immobilized. Your heart is reeling.

You've been hit, hard. Your heart is broken. It feels like your soul has been torn in two.

Your spouse is no longer here. This loss changes everything.

Take a deep breath. Again.

The Lord is here. He is with you in this.

Breathe.

———◆———

**God is our refuge and strength, an**
**ever-present help in trouble.**
**Psalm 46:1**

*Lord, I'm stunned, shocked, and shaken. Be my*
*strength and my help. You are my refuge.*

# 2

*I miss my mate desperately.*

*I look for them everywhere – in the living
room, kitchen, bathroom, and bedroom.*

*I think I hear that familiar voice. I spin around
and am shocked and disappointed all over again.*

*I feel devastated, crushed, shattered. My heart
is in pieces strewn all over the place.*

*I don't want to accept this. I can't.*

———◆———

Our hearts are designed to connect. We're created in the image
of God and wired for relationship.

When we marry, two become one. This bond is unique, deep,
and spiritual.

No wonder you look for your spouse. Your heart is searching.
You want them back. You want them here, now. Your heart is
yearning and longing for them.

Breathe. Slowly. Deeply.

The Lord knows your pain. He feels it. He is here.

———◆———

*"Before you were in your mother's womb, I knew you."*
*Jeremiah 1:5*

*Lord, You know me. My heart is crushed.*
*I can hardly breathe. I need You.*

# 3

*I wake up in the morning and suddenly realize all
over again that I'm alone. The shock and sadness
descend like a crushing weight on my chest.*

*The tears start to come, again. The heaviness
is stifling. I can barely breathe.*

*I push myself up on the side of the bed. I shake my head.*

*How can my love, my spouse, be gone?*

*My day has just begun, and I'm exhausted.
My heart feels so tired, so forlorn, so sad.*

*Sad. I'm so, so sad.*

---

Yes, this is sad – terribly sad. Missing your spouse is hard enough. Knowing that they're not coming back is gut-wrenching, even soul-tearing.

The weight on your heart is immense. Sadness is a natural result.

This sadness is healthy. Your heart is honoring your partner. You're expressing your love for them. You miss them deeply.

The Lord feels your sadness with you. He is closer than you know.

Breathe.

*Be merciful to me, Lord, for I am in distress; my eyes grow weak with sorrow, my soul and body with grief.*
**Psalm 31:9**

*Father, sorrow grips my heart. Be my comfort. Be my strength.*

# 4

*My emotions are so intense. I feel
drained, paralyzed, and confused.*

*Sometimes all I can do is cry. Other times, I'm so
sad that I can't seem to squeeze out a single tear.*

*Grief surrounds me like a little black cloud. It doesn't
matter what I'm doing or where I go, I carry it with me.*

*I can't think straight. My mind spins and
then freezes. My head feels so heavy.*

*I want to hear my spouse's voice so badly.*

———◈———

Grief is a moving target. It never stays still. It's always changing.

Your heart has been broken, perhaps even crushed. The grief is intense and runs deep – deeper than you can imagine.

Grieving the loss of a spouse is an emotional roller-coaster. There will be steep climbs, sudden curves, and disturbing drops. You'll be jostled about and thrown around quite a bit. It can be frustrating, confusing, and terrifying.

Your grief honors your mate. Your heart is expressing your love.

God created you to love. You're expressing the heart He gave you.

———◈———

*Be strong and take heart, all you
who hope in the Lord.*
*Psalm 31:24*

*Father, grief is confusing. The feelings are
intense. Strengthen me. Give me hope.*

# 5

*I miss my love, my soulmate. My heart is like
liquid and leaking out all over everything.*

*I try to be strong. When the grief comes, I try to fight it
off, put a good face on it, and be as normal as possible.*

*But things aren't normal. Nothing is
normal. Everything has changed.*

*I'm a mess. I can't seem to hold anything inside
for long. I feel sick inside, like some deep
part of me is broken and beyond repair.*

*I miss my spouse, and the missing is so intense.*

*I just want to withdraw and hide.*

---

Life has changed. The world suddenly feels empty, cold, unkind, and even dangerous.

You're created in the image of God. You're unique in human
history. There has never been another exactly like you, and
there never will be again.

The same is true of your spouse and marriage. Unique. Special.
Valuable beyond description. Priceless.

Your hearts were connected – two became one - and now one

heart is gone. Your heart has been torn. Grief is leaking out. This is natural and healthy.

The world isn't typically friendly to grieving hearts. It can be cold and unfeeling.

The Lord knows grief well. He knows you. He loves you and is walking with you in this mess. You are special to Him.

---

*I lift up my eyes to the mountains—where does my help come from? My help comes from the Lord, the Maker of heaven and earth.*
*Psalm 121:1-2*

*Lord, I feel broken. My heart is shattered. Speak to me. My help comes from You.*

# 6

*It was all so sudden. Here one moment and gone the next.*

*How does that happen? Why? What
am I supposed to do now?*

*I can't wrap my mind around it. My heart can't grasp it
somehow. I know it's true, but I can't seem to accept it.*

*I don't know what to do. I feel stuck, caught
between two worlds: what was and what is.*

*Please, can't things just go back to the way they were?*

No matter how death comes, it seems sudden even if it's anticipated. Life always departs in a single instant. This is especially
true when we lose a spouse.

Your love for your partner is so clear and evident. Of course,
your heart can't process this, at least not fully. Your mind is
trying to make sense of this somehow. It seems simple, but it's
not.

You're designed by God to love and be loved. When your heart
attaches, it clings. Love endures. You feel this tension. You love
your mate, but they're not here anymore.

God walks with you in this strange new place—this middle
ground of life not being what it was but not yet knowing what

it is now. Trust Him with your heart. Pour out your thoughts and feelings to Him. He loves you.

———◆◆◆———

*"The Lord himself goes before you and will be with you; He will never leave you nor forsake you. Do not be afraid; do not be discouraged."*
*Deuteronomy 31:8*

*Lord, I don't know how to think about this. You are with me. You never leave. Guard my heart from fear.*

# 7

*Life has become weird and strange.*

*My world has stopped. It's as if someone reached
down and pushed the pause button on my life.*

*The world around me, however, speeds on as
usual—as if nothing of consequence has happened.*

*My love, my partner is gone. How can this be?*

*I find myself getting angry about this. Life
suddenly seems cold and even cruel.*

*I don't like this at all.*

———◆———

Your life has changed forever. Your world has been altered. Almost everyone else's world, however, goes on much as before.

Your heart is feeling the disconnect between your personal world and the world at large. It feels wrong. No wonder you feel angry. Most grieving hearts do.

Daily life will be surreal for a while. Your life partner is gone. Everything has changed. You are part of the larger world out there, but right now you're unable to fully enter it.

That's okay. This "disconnect" is natural and common. It's as if you've been hit by a large truck. You're badly injured inside, hurt, and even crushed. The pain can be immense.

The Lord accepts you where you are. He holds your heart tenderly. He knows each thought and feeling. He is with you in this, all the way.

---

*But you, God, see the trouble of the afflicted;*
*you consider their grief and take it in hand.*
*Psalm 10:14*

*Father, you know my heart and my emotions.*
*You see my trouble. Help me to trust You.*

# 8

*I wish money wasn't such a big deal. Finances can be such a pain - so stressful.*

*My spouse is gone. I handle everything now. Bills keep coming. There are more expenses than I could have imagined.*

*I resent all the details and decisions - banks, social security, insurance, and all the rest. I need proof of this or that. I can't get into this or that account. So and so needs a death certificate. And so on...*

*I'm drowning in details.*

*I feel attacked and discouraged by these things. I'm frustrated, angry, and scared.*

---

Finances can be stressful even in settled times. When a spouse departs, costly details quickly descend upon us from every direction.

These details invade our grief and nip away at us. Decisions jab and poke our broken hearts. Our minds struggle under the weight of a to-do list we didn't want or ask for.

Breathe. Though frustrating, these financial matters are part of your grief journey. Let the emotions come. Freely share with the Lord what is happening inside you.

No matter what you're up against or what your financial situation, Jesus invites you to trust Him. He wants to work in and through you to accomplish His purposes in all this.

Let Jesus walk with you in these details and decisions. Stay with Him in the present moment. Rest in Him. He will direct your steps.

---

*Look at the birds of the air; they do not sow or reap or store away in barns, and yet your heavenly Father feeds them. Are you not much more valuable than they?*
*Matthew 6:26*

*Lord, amid all these frustrating details, I want to walk with You in the present moment. I trust You will direct my steps.*

# 9

*Anger. I don't like it — at all. However,*
*I'm feeling a lot of it lately.*

*I wonder, "Why?" more and more.*

*Why did it have to be my spouse? Why now?*
*Why this? Why us? Why this way?*

*Why?*

*All I get in return is silence. No answer.*

*Is there an answer?*

*I'm irritable and edgy. My fuse is shorter. I don't like this.*

*Yes, I'm angry.*

---

Sadness and anger are the two most common emotions we experience in grief. Feeling angry is natural, especially when we lose our life partner.

Anger itself is neutral. It's an emotion like any other emotion. It gets our attention because it can be so powerful. We know how anger is expressed can be destructive and harmful.

You were created for relationship and wired for connection. The marital bond is stunningly deep and intimate. When a spouse departs, it feels wrong. It's okay to be angry.

Breathe deeply. Ask God to give you ways to express anger that are healthy and healing. Write. Talk. Exercise. Draw. This is part of taking your grief—and your heart—seriously.

---

*"In your anger do not sin": Do not let the sun go down while you are still angry.*
*Ephesians 4:26*

*Lord, when I'm angry, guide me to express it in healthy ways. Use this anger to heal and mature me.*

# 10

*I feel nervous. I seem to be anxious all the time.*

*Sometimes, I find myself holding my breath.*
*Other times, I can't get enough air. It's like I'm*
*hyperventilating on a small scale, almost all the time.*

*I feel less safe now. My spouse is no longer here.*
*I feel vulnerable - like I'm always in danger.*

*I tremble sometimes. I can't think straight. My mind*
*wanders. My emotions are all over the place.*

*I wake up anxious. I walk around anxious. I go*
*through the day anxious. I go to bed at night anxious.*

*It's like I've been hijacked. Anxiety has*
*invaded and taken me hostage.*

---

Your world has changed. Someone you love deeply – your spouse and life partner - is no longer here. Everything is different now.

Your mind is attempting to understand this. Your heart has cracked open and emotion is spilling out. Many things seem uncertain. Anxiety is a natural result.

No one enjoys being anxious. We want to understand. We want peace of mind and heart.

The Lord is with you in this anxious, unknown territory you find yourself in. His arms are around you.

He invites you to breathe and to be patient with yourself. You're in uncharted territory. That can be unnerving and anxiety-producing.

Be kind to yourself. Rest in the Lord's embrace. Breathe.

*Search me, God, and know my heart; test me and know my anxious thoughts. See if there is any offensive way in me and lead me in the way everlasting.*
*Psalm 139:23-24*

*Father, You know my anxious thoughts. You are with me. In my anxiety, I look to You.*

# 11

*The anxiety is getting worse. Sometimes it takes over. My heart rate jumps. I nearly pass out. I can't catch my breath.*

*When it strikes, I'm terrified. Am I having panic attacks?*

*It's awful. Fear is growing inside me. I feel out of control. My emotions and body betray me.*

*On top of this, these episodes are embarrassing. I fall apart in public. I find myself afraid of going certain places or even of going out at all.*

*What's happening to me? Is something wrong? Am I going crazy?*

*I want my spouse back.*

———◆———

Anxiety and panic attacks are common in grief – and very common after the loss of spouse. This profound, deep loss naturally raises our usual anxiety baseline. We feel more nervous, less focused, and more vulnerable.

All this can be frightening. We don't feel like ourselves. We often feel overwhelmed and out of control. It's completely natural to wonder if we're losing it.

Anxiety and wondering about our sanity are part of the grief process. When the panic comes, breathe. Tell yourself, "I'm okay. This will pass."

You're not going crazy but losing someone you love has thrust you into what feels like an insane situation compared to your norm.

Acknowledge the anxiety and panic. The Lord is with you. Rest in Him. Share with Him. Be honest and real. He loves you.

---

*I waited patiently for the Lord; He turned to me and heard my cry. He lifted me out of the slimy pit, out of the mud and mire; He set my feet on a rock and gave me a firm place to stand.*
*Psalm 40:1-2*

*Lord, I feel like a mess. You are with me in this. Calm my heart. I trust You are guiding me through this.*

# 12

*I'm scared. I'm afraid of what might happen next.*

*It's dawning on me that almost anything can happen to anyone at any time. This includes me and everyone I love and care about. That's terrifying.*

*Suddenly, the world seems a very unsafe and dangerous place. I feel a little paranoid.*

*My spouse, my love, is gone. I naturally wonder, "Who's next?" I want to protect myself and those I love, but I don't know how. Perhaps I can't.*

*I'm stunned at how little I can control.*

*I feel helpless and scared.*

---

Fear can be a huge part of grief. When a spouse dies, it can trigger all kinds of hidden terrors. Life seems less safe and more threatening.

Fear will come knocking on the door of our hearts. When it does, we tend to do better when we acknowledge it and then feel our way through it. Trying to not be afraid only causes our minds to dwell more on the fear.

Express your fear to God. He knows already. He loves you and longs for you to talk with Him about what's happening inside you. Acknowledge the fear and get it out. Writing, talking, drawing, and even exercising can all be done in a spirit of prayer.

Share with God what you're feeling. Keep being honest and real with yourself and with Him.

---

*You are my hiding place; you will protect me from trouble and surround me with songs of deliverance.*
**Psalm 32:7**

*Lord, You know my fears. You are my hiding place. You protect me in ways I'm not aware of.*

# 13

*My mind is constantly spinning. I can't settle.*
*I can't rest. I'm having trouble sleeping.*

*I think of my love, my spouse. I think about*
*us and the way life used to be. I miss my*
*constant companion so desperately.*

*If I'm engaged in something or out with people, I seem to*
*do better. As soon as I'm alone, however, my brain goes*
*bonkers. My thoughts and feelings are all over the place.*

*It's like I'm on a mental merry-go-*
*round and I can't get off.*

*Restless. Unsettled. Anxious. Nervous.*
*I don't like this at all.*

---

When loss strikes, our minds get hit too. We're stunned. We try to figure out what happened and why. We wonder what will happen next, what we should be doing, and how all this is going to work out.

Our minds spin. Around and around. This is natural and common for grieving spouses.

Try slowing those thoughts down by writing or drawing. Get what you're thinking down on paper, no matter how ridiculous some of it might seem. Express it. Get it out.

God is with you, listening and guiding. Try writing to Him, openly and honestly.

The more you do this, the more manageable the mental treadmill will become.

---

*Yes, my soul, find rest in God;*
*my hope comes from Him.*
*Psalm 62:5*

*Father, bring peace to my mind. Cause me*
*to rest in You. You are my peace.*

# 14

*I'm all by myself now.*

*We were a pair. A couple. Spouses. Partners
in everything. Now, I'm alone.*

*I don't know what to do. I feel immobilized. I
wake up in the middle of the night terrified.*

*I walk around on hyper-alert. I experience
another loss of some kind almost every day.*

*I miss talking. I miss their voice. I miss their touch.
I miss their presence and companionship. I miss us.*

*My old life is gone, and now I have to
find a new one. How do I do that?*

---

Imagine two pieces of paper firmly glued together. To attempt to separate them would be disaster. When a spouse dies, the one left behind is torn and full of holes.

You carry your partner with you in many ways, even while their absence seems to permeate everything. Their physical presence is gone, and yet they are everywhere. Your heart is torn. Your life is full of holes. This is traumatic and painful.

You are created in the image of God and unique. So was your

spouse. Your marriage was one-of-a-kind. Your grief is unique and special, and that's also why it feels so lonely.

Your spouse is gone, but you are not alone. Jesus lives in you, and you live in Him. He shares your loneliness and feels your pain. He whispers comfort and peace to you through His Word, nature, safe people, and some circumstances.

*"Never will I leave you; never will I forsake you."*
*Hebrews 13:5*

*Lord, You are still with me. You know me. You love me. I look to You in my pain and distress.*

# 15

*I feel rejected.*

*My friends have changed, especially the couples.
They're avoiding me. They don't call, text or
email anymore. They don't invite me out.*

*I don't fit in anymore. I'm widowed. I'm not one of them.*

*When I see couples, grief surges up within
me. My spouse is gone. I'm alone now.*

*These people used to be my friends. I have so many
wonderful memories of my spouse and me with them.*

*Now, it's like I have some contagious disease.*

*I'm mad, frustrated, confused, and hurt. I feel
like everything I had has been taken from me
and I keep losing more along the way.*

———◆———

Couples have couple relationships and couple friends. When we lose a spouse, our entire relational network is upended. This is natural, and even inevitable in many cases. But it's also frustrating, confusing, and painful.

You've been thrust into a new world that looks the same but where all the rules are different. You might feel abandoned, rejected, and even betrayed. The pain can strike deep and begin to plant seeds of bitterness inside you.

The Lord knows all about being an outcast. He continually experiences rejection. He's also an expert at forgiveness.

Jesus, the Forgiving Outcast, lives in you. He understands. He loves you. He can also empower you to forgive so that your heart is not repeatedly crushed by what others might say or do.

He knows. He gets it. Cry out to Him.

*"So do not fear, for I am with you; do not be dismayed, for I am your God. I will strengthen you and help you; I will uphold you with my righteous right hand."*
*Isaiah 41:10*

*Lord, you live in me. You will never leave me or abandon me. Fill me and empower me to forgive.*

# 16

*How do I parent now – by myself?*

*There are no more conversations with my spouse
about what to do. I have no backup for parenting
decisions or guidance. Everything I do with
the kids just amplifies my mate's absence.*

*Then I look ahead. Birthdays. Holidays. Proms.
Graduations. Marriages. Grandchildren. My
spouse won't be there. It will just be me.*

*I suddenly feel sick.*

*I'm doing the parenting work of two, while grieving.
Life seems merciless. It drags us all forward
with our hearts strewn in pieces behind us.*

*I feel abandoned and alone. How do I do this?*

---

We love our kids and want the best for them. Until recently, you tackled the challenge of parenting together with your spouse. As you said, everything now falls on you. The sense of responsibility can be overwhelming.

In addition, you get to parent from a broken, aching heart. You were stretched and stressed before. Now life might seem impossible.

Here's one huge truth to remember: God is your Father. He is the perfect parent. He lives in you. Strictly speaking, you are far from alone in this.

God wants to parent your kids through you. You are a channel of His life and wisdom to them. You're a reflection of Him as their ultimate parent. The goal is not that you would be a perfect parent, but that your kids experience the love of Christ through you during this time.

Breathe deeply. See Jesus in front of you. Feel His arms around you. Ask Him to live through you to your children.

Your only task is to walk with God in the present moment. He loves you. He is always at work.

———◦———

*I keep my eyes always on the Lord. With him*
*at my right hand, I will not be shaken.*
*Psalm 16:8*

*Lord, You are the ultimate parent. Live through me*
*and parent the children You have given me. Help*
*me to walk with You in the present moment.*

# 17

*My adult children don't understand.*
*They won't let me grieve.*

*They keep trying to take care of me. They keep giving*
*advice I haven't asked for. I feel nagged and smothered.*

*I know they're worried about me. They want*
*me to be okay. I will be okay, but I don't*
*feel okay yet – not by a long shot.*

*I miss my love, my spouse. I need to talk about them,*
*share, and vent. I wish my kids could just listen.*

*None of us knows what to do. We're all hurting.*

———◆———

Loss can be complicated, and confusing. You're right. Our adult children don't know what to do with this any more than we do.

With your spouse gone, you're the only parent they have left. That can be terrifying. No wonder they want you to be okay. They're trying to protect you, but in this case, it ends up backfiring.

Yes, you need to grieve. You need to express your grief. Your heart needs to be heard and appreciated.

Even if your adult kids are uncomfortable with it, as you grieve openly and honestly, you're modeling for them what healthy grieving looks like. This is a huge life skill that they will need again and again.

The Lord is listening. He is love. He is healing you in ways you're not aware of. Ask Him for His wisdom in relating to your kids. He knows all about parenting.

We never stop being parents, even when we're grieving the loss of our soulmate. Ask the Lord to work in and through you to bring comfort and healing to your family during this time.

———◆———

*A father to the fatherless, a defender of widows, is God in His holy dwelling. God sets the lonely in families...*
**Psalm 68:5-6**

*Lord, you know our hearts. Heal my family. Give me wisdom and comfort. Give us grace to walk with You through this valley.*

# 18

*My mind is foggy. I can hardly think. I
forget things. My head feels heavy.*

*I go out into the world, but it's like I'm not there.
Everything looks the same, but everything feels different.*

*Everything **is** different. My soulmate
is gone, and I'm alone now.*

*I'm exhausted. My sleep pattern is off. I can't stop
thinking about my love, my mate. Memories assault me.*

*I want my old life back. I don't like this new one. It's
painful, confusing, exhausting, and desperately lonely.*

---

Mental fog and fatigue are common in grief. Our spouse has departed, and life is not the same. Our lives and hearts are not the same. This is all too much for our brains. We shift into maintenance mode.

Again, it's like being hit by a truck. We're stunned and immobilized. While we recover, our minds are foggy. Our thinking is less sharp. Loss packs a cognitive wallop.

Please don't expect yourself to cruise through this unaffected. Your thinking, work performance, and energy will naturally be impacted. You are not yourself right now. Life is not the same.

You are not the same. You don't have to be on the top of your game to experience God, heal, recover, and grow. Accept yourself where you are, as you are. God does. He is kind to you. Be kind to yourself.

---

*I went about mourning as though for
my friend or brother. I bowed my head
in grief as though weeping for my mother.*
**Psalm 35:14**

*Lord, I'm exhausted. I feel like a shadow of
my former self. Support me. Sustain me.*

# 19

*Food doesn't taste the same. Frankly, I don't want to eat.*

*Sometimes I end up skipping meals because I simply forget to eat. I'm not hungry. I have no appetite. When I do eat, nothing tastes good.*

*Plus, eating alone is painful. Every meal reminds me my soulmate is no longer here.*

*Nothing seems to feel good either. Perhaps I'm growing numb.*

*What's happening to me?*

*Life as I knew it has disappeared. Maybe I disappeared along with it.*

———◆———

The loss of a spouse pounds our entire system. The resulting grief strikes our taste buds too. We find ourselves eating mechanically – not for pleasure, but for survival.

Some have no appetite and eat less and less. Others eat more and more. Grief tends to drive us one way or the other. When death strikes our life partner, parts of us seem to die too.

As you process your grief in healthy ways, your appetite will eventually return. Over time, things will most likely even out again, but they will not be the same as before. Life has changed now. Your world has been forever altered.

Tell the Lord about this. Share your heart with Him. Even if you don't feel His presence, He's there.

---

*As the deer pants for streams of water,*
*so my soul pants for you, my God.*
**Psalm 42:1**

*Lord, remind me that now is not forever. Though*
*I feel stuck, I trust that You are at work.*

# 20

*Someone asked me yesterday what I miss the most.*

*Most of all, I miss my mate's presence.*

*A person's presence is more powerful than I dreamed.*
*No matter where I look, my love is not there.*
*Only in pictures, videos, and in the memories*
*buried in my heart. Their presence is gone.*

*My life and world feel so empty. Half my heart is gone.*
*I limp through the day, going through the motions.*

*Their absence permeates everything.*

---

A person's presence is powerful indeed. When we're with someone we love, our hearts respond. We feel safe. We drop our guard a bit. We become real and authentic.

When a life companion and partner departs, the hole they leave is immense. We become hyperaware of their absence. We can't see them or be with them. Our hearts long for them. We mourn.

When we lose a spouse, the whole world can seem empty.

God wired your heart for relationships. You were created to love and be loved. You were one with your spouse. No wonder this hurts.

*Brothers and sisters, we do not want you
to be uninformed about those who sleep
in death, so that you do not grieve like the
rest of mankind, who have no hope.*
*1 Thessalonians 4:13*

*Father, I miss my spouse so much. Even
though the loss hurts, thank you for love.
Thank you for placing them in my life.*

# 21

*I've thought more about what I miss the most.*

*It's not just my spouse's presence. It's everything. I miss everything about them – and about us.*

*I miss their voice, their smile, and their laughter. I miss their touch. I miss all that we had and all that we had planned on. I even miss the quirks that frustrated me so much.*

*I miss them. I miss everything about them. My heart is broken and aching. The pain is excruciating.*

*I don't know how to do this.*

---

When a spouse dies, we lose not only the person but also everything attached to them. These losses hit us, again and again, over time. It can seem like we discover a new loss almost every day.

The grief is heavy, even crushing sometimes. I think of Job in the Old Testament. He experienced multiple, heavy losses, all on top of each other. Sudden. Traumatic. Devastating. His losses would have killed most of us.

He felt the pain. He was emotionally overwhelmed and physically debilitated. He had questions—lots of them. In the midst of it all, he did what he knew to do.

He expressed his grief. He kept presenting his broken, shattered heart to the One who created him. He clung to God.

---

*My eyes have grown dim with grief;*
*my whole frame is but a shadow.*
***Job 17:7***

*Lord, cause me to be honest and open with You.*
*You know it all already, and You love me.*

# 22

*Work is a challenge now, and that's an understatement.*

*I'm going through the motions. I'm only half there at best. Sometimes, I don't think I'm there at all.*

*I can't think straight. My mind wanders. My thoughts keep coming back to my spouse. I'm in a fog most of the day.*

*Work distracts me from my grief, and yet grief enters my work at the same time. I wear my loss wherever I go. I know coworkers are watching. I can feel it.*

*Just getting out of bed is a chore. Work feels like a solo climb of Mount Everest.*

*No matter where I am, I feel alone.*

---

The loss of a spouse affects every part of life because it strikes us at the core of our being. Our souls shake. Drastic, traumatic change has occurred and now it is trickling down to every part of our existence.

Work is, of course, a huge challenge. Life is not business as usual. Your heart, mind, soul, and body are all powerfully impacted by this terrible loss. Your work will be too.

Yes, other people are watching. That's okay. You can't change that. You can only take care of you. Focus on taking your heart seriously. Invest your time and energy in grieving in healthy ways.

Good self-care is not selfish. Taking care of yourself is one way to honor your spouse and love those around you. In fact, a healthy you is one of the best gifts you can give to others.

The Lord will guide and teach you. He's providing for you each and every moment. Good self-care begins with resting in Him.

*Trust in the Lord with all your heart. Don't lean on your own understanding. In all your ways acknowledge Him, and He will direct your paths.*
*Proverbs 3:5-6*

*Father, guide and empower me at work. Live through me, even in this time of heaviness. Keep my eyes on You.*

# 23

*Where did everyone go?*

*First, my spouse died. Then everyone
else began disappearing.*

*So many said they would be here for me. Where are they?*

*Lots of promises of support, but no follow
through. No calls, texts, emails. Nothing.*

*Is there something wrong with me? Have
I contracted a contagious disease?*

*I've never asked much of anything from others. Now,
when I need them, they're nowhere to be found.*

*My love's death was more than enough.
I hadn't counted on this too.*

---

If it helps any, what you're experiencing is all too common.
Grieving spouses often feel isolated and even rejected. At first,
we get inundated with condolences and attention, and then
poof—nothing.

Most people give us about a month to grieve, and then they
expect us to be back to our normal selves. The problem is that
we're not who we were. We're different now. Our world has
changed. Deep loss has changed us.

People don't know what to do with grief. No wonder grief is so lonely.

God understands. He is probably the most misunderstood, ignored, and rejected Being in the universe. He knows all about this kind of relational pain.

He shares your loneliness with you. He knows your confusion, frustration, and pain. His love for you is beyond measure.

———◄❈►———

*And so we know and rely on the love*
*God has for us. God is love.*
*1 John 4:16*

*When I feel alone, Lord, let me remember You. I rely on your love for me.*

# 24

*Couples seem to be everywhere. Talking,
eating, holding hands, kissing.*

*Social media doesn't help. Couples are everywhere
there, too. Couples celebrating anniversaries,
traveling together, and enjoying life and each other.
Nothing but smiles and happiness everywhere.*

*And here I am. Alone. Widowed. Grieving.*

*I'm beginning to dread going out.
I'm alone everywhere I go.*

*I'm not who I was. I don't know who I am.
My spouse is gone, but I still feel married.*

*I guess everything reminds me of my loss. I
love my spouse. I miss them terribly.*

---

Seeing other couples can be painful. The grief can well up and
burst out without warning. This is natural. You're a widowed
spouse living in what seems to be a world of twosomes. Every
couple can be a reminder of what was and will be no more.

Feeling alone and lonely is part of grieving the loss of a spouse.
Seeing other couples isn't pleasant, but it gives you an opportu-
nity to express the love and grief inside you.

Breathe. Let the grief come. Feel it. Acknowledge it. Share your heart openly with the Lord. Try not to hold anything back. He gets it. Jesus knows all about loneliness.

Ask God to bring people into your life who will accept and love you as you are. Trust Him with this. He knows who and what you need.

———⬥———

*Trust in the Lord with all your heart and lean not on your own understanding; in all your ways submit to Him, and He will make your paths straight.*
*Proverbs 3:5-6*

*Lord, I accept that seeing other couples is hard.*
*Work in me to use this pain and loneliness for*
*your purposes. Heal me. Provide for me.*

# 25

*Today, I'm discovering that I'm angry with God.*

*I've been hiding this. I've been scared to admit it. I know I shouldn't be angry with Him, but I am. After all, He could have done something. He could have stopped this. He could have healed my spouse.*

*Instead, He let them die. I feel like He took them away—from me and everyone else who loved them.*

*I don't understand. I don't get it. It doesn't make sense. I'll never understand. All the clichés I hear mean nothing.*

*God, why?*

———◆———

Questioning God in times of loss is natural, and especially so when a beloved spouse dies. Most widowed spouses get angry with Him at some point in their grief journey.

We want our mate, companion, and life partner back. We're angry. Anger looks for a target. For most of us, the buck stops with God.

God is well acquainted with anger. He knows our hearts and minds. He knows our distress and frustration. He is not surprised by anything we think or feel.

Since God already knows you're angry, try expressing your

anger to Him. Be honest. Be real. Don't hold back. God knows your heart. He can handle it.

Pray it out. Write it out. Talk out loud to Him. Begin to make it a habit to express what you're thinking and feeling to Him without reservation. Share your heart as fully and completely as possible.

God wants and longs for you to share your heart with Him. He loves you.

------◆------

*My eyes are dim with grief. I call to you, Lord, every day; I spread out my hands to you.*
*Psalm 88:9*

*God, I'm angry. I have questions. You know my heart. Help me to be real with You.*

# 26

*I can't believe what people will say. If I hear, "At least they're in a better place," or "At least you had them this long," or at least anything one more time, I'm going to scream.*

*People don't see me, do they? What are they thinking? Don't they know how bad I'm hurting?*

*I'm concluding that other people just don't get it. They don't understand. Maybe they can't.*

*First, they disappear. Then, when I do see them, they utter niceties and platitudes.*

*Not helpful. Not helpful at all.*

---

You're right. People don't understand. Unless they've been there themselves, the best they can do is sympathize. They feel uncomfortable. They don't know what to say, so they end up saying what they've heard others say.

People don't like pain. When they suddenly find themselves in the presence of suffering, they don't know what to do. It would be nice if they simply stayed silent, but few manage to do this.

What people say is far more about them than it is about you. Out of the mouth, the heart speaks. Try not to make their words about you. What they say is about them.

God is the ultimate listener. In fact, He's perfect at it. He's listening to your heart now. He feels your pain and frustration.

You won't get clichés and platitudes from Him. You'll get His constant presence and His eternal love.

*"I have heard many things like these; you
are miserable comforters, all of you!
Job 16:2*

*People don't understand, but You do, Lord.
You know me. You love me. Comfort me.*

# 27

*I feel confused.*

*I know what happened. I know I miss my spouse
terribly. I know I feel alone in my grief.*

*I don't know what life looks like now. I don't
know what's ahead. I keep trying to figure things
out, but my mind ends up going in circles. I'm
stuck on a treadmill, and I can't step off.*

*I don't know what to do. I don't know how to feel.
I don't know what to say. Everything has changed.
It feels like I'm in a free fall with no safety net.*

*I notice I hang my head a lot. I sigh continually. I want
this to be over, but I have no idea what that means.*

*I want my spouse back, but I know
that's not going to happen.*

*I'm confused.*

---

Loss this deep brings so much change with it. In some senses,
it changes everything. The ripple effects are pervasive and stunning. Nothing in our lives is left untouched.

Our minds try to make sense of it. Our hearts are wired for

connection. Separation like this doesn't compute. We know it happens, but that doesn't mean we can easily accept it.

Again, you're in uncharted territory. You've had other losses, but the loss of a spouse is different. You've never been here before. The landscape is unfamiliar. You don't know what's coming next.

Confusion would be natural, and it is common in grief. Nothing quite makes sense the way it used to.

The Lord knows. He knows the path ahead. Lean into Him and let Him lead, one step at a time.

---

*But now, Lord, what do I look*
*for? My hope is in you.*
**Psalm 39:7**

*Lord, you know my confusion. I will express my*
*thoughts, worries, and fears to You. Let me hold*
*nothing back. You are my hope and safety.*

# 28

*Where is God in all this?*

*Yes, I know He's with me. He's with everyone. He's everywhere. He can do anything. He cares for me. I know all these things, but somehow, I don't feel them. I wonder if I feel much of anything.*

*I guess I'm still angry with Him. Or perhaps I just don't understand. I know I'm holding back. I feel like I'm distancing my heart from Him. Either that or He's disappeared on me like everyone else.*

*I want to know why this happened.
Why did my spouse have to die?*

*If God would tell me why, then perhaps I could let this go. Maybe then I could see some good that might come out of it. Right now, I see nothing good at all.*

*Yes, I'm still angry with Him.*

———◆———

Thank you for being honest and sharing your heart. Thank you for expressing your grief openly. For most of us, the pain of the loss of our spouse causes us to question many things, even God Himself.

Many of us distance ourselves from God in our confusion and pain. We hunger to understand. When we need to know something and can't seem to figure it out on our own, we ask an expert. God is the expert on all things, so we naturally bring our questions to Him.

If we sense silence, it hurts. We can feel like He doesn't care. As a result, we can feel more alone and even more devastated.

Keep being honest with Him. Though you might pull away from Him, He will never pull away from you. Express your heart. Be real. Grieve.

---

*Why, my soul, are you downcast? Why so disturbed within me? Put your hope in God, for I will yet praise Him, my Savior and my God.*
**Psalm 42:5**

*Lord, You feel far away. I'm angry, and I don't know what to think. I fear my heart is shutting down. Help.*

# 29

*All this has made me think of my own mortality.*

*My love, my mate, died. I'm going to die. We're all going to die. None of us escapes this.*

*That's terrifying. And it could happen anytime, anywhere, to anyone. To me.*

*I wonder if I'm getting paranoid. I don't feel like myself at all. I hate this fear.*

*Am I going crazy? I know I've asked that before.*

*My heart is shaking.*

---

The loss of someone we love, and especially the death of a spouse, brings many things home to us. Our own mortality is one of them. The old saying is true: "Everyone wants to go to heaven, but no one wants to die."

The biggest issue for most people is the feeling of uncertainty and lack of control. It's like the proverbial carpet has been pulled out from under us. We find ourselves wondering about almost everything. Our world has been shaken, and we're trembling inside as a result.

No, you're not crazy. Most grieving hearts experience this. You need reassurance. We all do. God is good at this. This is what

His word and His promises are all about. He reassures us of who He is and who we are. He is our shepherd. He provides and leads. He knows our fears. He meets us in our messes.

Breathe. You are not alone. You are not crazy. You will get through this.

————◆————

*On my bed I remember you; I think of you through the watches of the night. Because you are my help, I sing in the shadow of your wings. I cling to you; your right hand upholds me.*
*Psalm 63:6-8*

*God, I'm terrified of what might happen next. I need your reassurance. I cling to You.*

# 30

*I feel guilty.*

*I find myself thinking about what I should have said and could have done. I regret things I said and did. I ask, "What if..." I wonder, "If only..."*

*The guilt is heavy. I feel terrible about myself. I feel like I'm coming apart. Suddenly, I can't seem to do anything right. I'm embarrassed and ashamed. I want to hide.*

*And I can't make any of it right.*

*My spouse is gone. What do I do with this? Can I do anything?*

*I feel like I'm punishing myself, and I can't seem to stop.*

---

After the death of our life partner, we wonder about what we could have done and didn't, or what we did that we wish we hadn't. This is natural and common. Yet, guilt is not our friend.

Guilt only leads to shame. It produces nothing good. It keeps us looking at ourselves. Guilt boxes us in and then keeps us imprisoned.

Release yourself. If there are things you need to ask forgiveness for, do that. Confession is good for the soul. Receive God's forgiveness. His mercy and grace are always there, waiting for you.

Jesus Christ died for your sins and mine. The debt has been paid in full. It is finished. Nothing you have ever done, or could ever do or neglect to do, is stronger than Jesus' sacrifice. His cross conquered our sin. He knows. He forgives. He releases from guilt.

Think on this. See Jesus in front of you. Walk into His arms and rest. His acceptance is perfect.

---

*Therefore, there is now no condemnation for those who are in Christ Jesus.*
**Romans 8:1**

*God, I release this guilt to You. If it returns, I'll release it again. I rest in your acceptance and love.*

# 31

*I'm exhausted.*

*I'm doing what I know to do to take care of myself, but
I'm still walking around in a fog. I can't think straight.
My sleep isn't what it was. My energy level is down.*

*I drag myself out of bed. I drag myself around
and out. I drag myself through work and errands.
Everywhere I go, I'm alone – even in a crowd.*

*I drag myself back home. I stare at walls. I blip
out. Time passes, and I wonder where it went.*

*I'm tired all the time. Is there something
wrong with me? Am I sick?*

*Maybe I need to see a doctor.*

---

Fatigue is the number one physical symptom of grief, especially with the loss of a spouse. Your entire system is getting
hit by this loss. After a while, your mind and body shift into
maintenance mode. There is no energy for anything else.

When loss strikes, grief is the result. Grief enters our lives and
takes up an enormous amount of space. Mental space. Emotional space. Spiritual space. There's much less of us available
to do routine life. For most of us, normal life is demanding

enough. Loss throws a grenade into all this. It stuns us and turns life upside down.

Doing life takes even more energy than before. After all, you're alone now in many ways. It's just you dealing with the responsibilities and details of life. Fatigue is the result. Exhaustion is natural and common.

If you're concerned about your health, get checked out. Seeing a doctor during challenging times is always a good idea.

In the Bible, people in grief often expressed exhaustion. No wonder. We're wired for connection and created for relationship. Loss taxes us greatly.

Rest as best as you can. God can handle your life. Let Him be your life today.

---

*The Lord is my shepherd, I lack nothing. He makes me lie down in green pastures, He leads me beside quiet waters, He refreshes my soul.*
*Psalm 23:1-2*

*Lord, I can barely lift my head. Restore and refresh me. Manage my routine. You are my shepherd.*

# 32

*I guess everyone expects me to be over this.*

*Get over my spouse? Ridiculous.*

*Every time I mention my love's name, people grow quiet. They look uncomfortable. They change the subject. They excuse themselves and disappear.*

*And I'm left there, alone in my grief. I sometimes wonder if anyone cares.*

*I sense that some people are avoiding me altogether. What do I do with that?*

*No one likes grief, I guess.*

*Can't people see how badly I'm hurting? Can't they just accept me where I am?*

---

You're right. The world doesn't like grief. People don't know what to do with it. Few people can handle being in the presence of suffering for long.

We all experience loss. We're designed to be loving and supportive of each other. Yet most of us choose personal comfort over meeting people where they are in their pain.

Thankfully, the Lord is an expert at this. He is well acquainted with loss, suffering, grief, and pain. For those who are willing,

He can train them to be compassionate conveyers of His love and care.

Perhaps you could be such a vessel—a reflection of His love, hope, and healing to this wounded world.

There are people out there who get it. They are safe and compassionate. Look for them. Ask God to bring them into your life.

———◆———

*I hope in the Lord Jesus to send Timothy to you soon, that I also may be cheered when I receive news about you. I have no one else like Him, who will show genuine concern for your welfare.*
*Philippians 2:19-20*

*Lord, I feel so alone now. Send me a few people like Timothy. Provide companions for me on this journey.*

# 33

*I'm having trouble finding supportive people. I've gotten enough weird looks and blank stares.*

*I expected kindness and compassion. Instead, people I counted on are disappearing.*

*I'm keeping more to myself. I'm starting to pull back and grieve in private. This feels safer.*

*But I also feel alone – so alone. And angry.*

*I'm sad it's this way. Shouldn't it be different? Shouldn't we be loving and supportive to one another?*

*I try to trust, and then I get disappointed. How do I know whom to share with and whom not to?*

*My heart is fragile. Every conversation feels risky. I miss my spouse.*

---

If it helps any, what you're describing is common. Many grieving spouses experience this. Most people don't know what to do with intense grief.

We all need safe people in our lives. A safe person meets us where we are. They don't judge. They don't try to fix. They listen.

Safe people have no personal agenda for you or your life. Their only goal is to love you where you are, as you are. In most cases, they are people who have known significant loss and pain, perhaps even the loss of their spouse.

The Lord places these people around us, though we may not know them yet. He invites us to trust Him with what we need. Ask. Seek. Knock.

---

*So I say to you: Ask and it will be given to you; seek and you will find; knock and the door will be opened to you. For everyone who asks receives; the one who seeks finds; and to the one who knocks, the door will be opened.*
**Luke 11:9-10**

*Lord, bring safe people into my life. Lead me to them. I ask, seek, and knock.*

# 34

*Where are these safe people that you talk about? It seems like everyone I encounter either runs away or tries to fix me.*

*How do you fix the loss of a spouse?*

*Where are the ones who will listen? Where are those who will ask about my spouse and let me share their story? My heart is full and burdened. I want to share, but I'm having trouble finding anyone I feel safe with.*

*Yes, a journal is good. Writing and talking out loud to myself help. But I need people too. I need hugs and touch amid all this.*

*I believe there are safe people out there. I want to find them. What can I do?*

---

Your struggle is a common one. Safe people are rare indeed, but they're out there.

I believe that God brings us the people we need—or brings us to them. He knows. Amid the pain and grief, we look up and seek. We ask for these people. Provide for us, Lord.

I've found that the best way to find safe, supportive people is to become one myself. Safe, compassionate people are drawn to each other like magnets. They intuitively seem to recognize one another.

In your grief, try focusing on being safe for others. Put aside judgment. Observe. Listen. Don't fix. Enter their world and spend a few moments with them there.

The Lord will bless this. He will empower you. He can do this in and through you. And you'll sense His presence and love in it.

---

*Do to others as you would have them do to you.*
*Luke 6:31*

*Lord, live through me and express your*
*love to others. I feel so empty, but You are*
*limitless. Make me a safe person.*

# 35

*Sometimes, I seem to be doing better, and
then I get hit again. The grief comes and
smacks me, seemingly out of nowhere.*

*A song. A familiar place. A picture. A certain aroma.
A sudden memory. Anything can set me off.*

*The grief wells up inside me so quickly. It feels like
I'm going to burst if I don't let it out somehow.*

*When this happens in public, I feel embarrassed,
scared, and a little crazy. Is this normal?*

*I miss my spouse. What do I do with this?*

---

Grief bursts. We all have them. We're minding our own business, and something triggers us. Grief falls upon us like an anvil.

Anything can trigger us. Anytime. Anywhere.

This can cause us to live in fear, as if we're always walking on eggshells, waiting for the next grief attack. We shift from living to protecting ourselves.

This is extremely common for grieving spouses, and it can be so frustrating. When the grief hits, breathe. Breathe deeply and slowly. Remember the Lord is with you, right then, in that moment.

He feels your grief. Lean into Him. And breathe.

———◆———

> **We wait in hope for the Lord; He
> is our help and our shield.**
> **Psalm 33:20**

*Lord, I accept that grief bursts will come. When the
emotion hits, cause me to look to You and rest in You.
You are my shield. I am safe and secure in You.*

# 36

*Nights are hard – so hard. The tears*
*flow almost every night.*

*As I lay there thinking, the memories come flooding*
*in. I can almost feel my spouse, my love, next to me.*

*I miss their embrace. I keep dreaming of*
*one more conversation, one more kiss.*

*The bedroom has become the loneliest place in my world.*

*This is so painful.*

*How strange life is now.*

———◈———

The pain and loneliness are stifling. The longing can be intense. The marriage bond is deep and intimate. It involves our whole being – mind, body, soul, and spirit.

We hunger for deep, soul-connected intimacy. When we have it, our souls delight. When we don't, our hearts ache. For a bereaved spouse, the bedroom can be one of the most challenging places on earth.

Desperate for relief, some seek solace in the arms of another. Afterwards, however, the loneliness usually returns with a vengeance, with guilt and feelings of unfaithfulness following closely behind.

You need time to grieve. If you reach out for companionship too soon, the new relationship may end up being about replacing what you had rather than about the two people involved. Take your time.

God is never in a hurry. He invites you to wait on Him and allow Him to bring healing before prematurely seeking a new relationship.

Keep breathing deeply. Pay attention to your heart. Keep processing your grief in healthy ways. The Lord will guide you in this. Allow Him to order your days and direct your paths.

He knows your needs and desires. He is good. He loves you.

———◆———

*Turn to me and be gracious to me,*
*for I am lonely and afflicted.*
*Psalm 25:16*

*Lord, guard my heart. You know my needs*
*and my longings. You live in me. I trust*
*You to heal me, one step at a time.*

# 37

*I want to talk again about these grief bursts.*

*I'm scared. I dread the next one. I'm pulling back more. My heart is going into hiding.*

*Is there a way I can prepare for grief bursts, even though I never know when they will happen or what will trigger them?*

*It seems I'm in flight mode all the time. I fear I'm shutting down in order to try and keep myself under control.*

*I long for my love, my partner. I don't like this new life.*

---

Fear can be such a large part of grief, especially when we lose a spouse. If we get hit enough, we start bracing for future blows rather than living in the present.

Yes, you can proactively prepare for grief bursts. Imagine yourself in a public place and suddenly the grief strikes. What will you do? What are your options? What do you want to be able to do?

You could breathe deeply and make your way to someplace more private. If you're talking to someone, you could excuse yourself. You could breathe deeply where you are and see how you do. There may be some cases where you can stay and continue after a pause.

The key is to take your heart seriously and do what's best for you. Ask the Lord for guidance in this. Go through it in your mind and decide beforehand how you will handle it.

You're right. Grief bursts will come. The Lord knows and is not surprised by them. He is with you in them. Decide with Him how you will approach them.

———◆———

*Guide me in your truth and teach me, for you are God my Savior, and my hope is in you all day long.*
**Psalm 25:5**

*God, I give my fear to You. Give me ability to feel the fear and then let it pass on through. Guide and teach me.*

# 38

*I thought my family would understand. I guess not.*

*Some are supportive. Others seem impatient. They look at me with eyes that say, "Come on. Get over it. Move on."*

*Really? We're talking about my spouse, my love, my life partner. Get over it? Impossible.*

*I had counted on family to be there for me. This is disappointing, and painful.*

*This loss impacts them too. I don't understand why they're acting this way. Don't they care?*

*I know they love me, but most of them aren't helpful right now. I find myself hiding more when I'm with them.*

---

Many widowed spouses find family to be less than supportive. They're compassionate for a while, but if our grief lasts for more than a month, they wonder what's wrong with us.

This impacts us greatly. We long to be seen, heard, and understood, especially when we're in pain. Family should be the best and safest place to grieve openly and freely. But often this is not the case.

For the sake of our own hearts, we may need to lower our expectations of those around us, including family. Rather than risk growing bitter, it's best to forgive quickly, and then keep forgiving as necessary.

The Lord understands. He hears and knows your heart. Jesus' own family didn't understand Him, His mission, or why He did what He did. You're in good company. Immerse yourself in Him.

---

*Be kind and merciful to each other, forgiving one another, just as God in Christ has forgiven you.*
*Ephesians 4:32*

*Lord, love my family through me. Protect my heart from hurt and damage. Enable me to be real and to forgive quickly when I'm disappointed.*

# 39

*Family members aren't the only ones who are less than supportive right now. I sense my coworkers are starting to roll their eyes. They stop talking when I come near. I feel like a leper.*

*I smile and fake it. It's easier this way. I cry alone. My grief has become a private thing. I guess most people prefer it that way.*

*No wonder I feel alone in all this, even while surrounded by people that I know care about me. At least, I think they care about me.*

*I find myself being sarcastic and morose, but I try to hide that too. I'm talking to myself most of the time. I don't trust anyone else to listen.*

*Why did my spouse have to go? This is so, so hard.*

---

Good listeners can be hard to find at times. Although we all know grief, few people process it well. We tend to shove our grief down deep inside, only to have it leak out in anger, frustration, anxiety, and depression. This is especially true when we lose a spouse.

Keep breathing deeply. Keep finding ways to express the pain and grief. Write it out. Talk it out—even out loud to yourself. Draw or paint it out. Exercise it out.

The workplace is notorious for ignoring grief. Performance is expected. Work colleagues will be compassionate and support-ive at first, but that quickly fades into the background because, "We have work to do."

The Lord is with you at work. He goes before you. He sits with you and walks with you. He is always working. He is your con-stant companion. See Him at your workplace. Talk to Him. Unload the pain and frustration to Him.

---

*Hannah replied, "I am a woman who is deeply troubled...I was pouring out my soul to the Lord...I have been praying here out of my great anguish and grief."*
*1 Samuel 1:15-16*

*Lord, You are my strength. Live through me and empower me to do all You call me to. Let me see You in my work.*

# 40

*I seem to be forgetting things more. Where
I put stuff. Why I came into the room.
What I was doing. Where I was going.*

*I forget appointments. I can't remember what
day it is. It's like my brain is going numb.*

*It's scary. What's happening to me? Is this grief?
Of course, I imagine the worst. Do I have a
brain tumor? Mental illness? Dementia?*

*My partner is gone. No one is looking out for
me, at least not in the same way. I'm starting
to worry. Is this going to get better?*

———

Grief from the loss of a spouse hits our entire being with
incredible force. The mental and cognitive affects can be
disturbing.

We forget things. We blip out. We go blank and stare at walls.
This is natural and common.

You are a closed system. You have only so much mental space.
When deep grief like this invades, it gobbles up a lot of mental
real estate. Simply put, you have less brain available for every-
day functioning.

The result is usually increased forgetfulness and decreased

mental energy and focus. As you continue to process the grief within, these mental challenges will most likely improve over time. If you're concerned, however, please see your doctor.

Lay these things before the Lord. Express your fears, doubts, and concerns. He is listening. He is protecting you and providing for you, even if you don't feel His presence sometimes. Rest in Him. He is working for your good.

---

*That is why, for Christ's sake, I delight in weaknesses, in insults, in hardships, in persecutions, in difficulties. For when I am weak, then I am strong.*
*2 Corinthians 12:10*

*Lord, even if I'm far from at my best, You are at work in and through me. I am loved. I am safe and secure. You know my heart. I rest in You.*

# 41

*I had a panic attack today.*

*A cloud of anxiety came upon me at work.
My heart raced. I felt lightheaded. My vision
narrowed. Everything closed in on me. I started
hyperventilating. The panic I felt was awful.*

*I sat for a moment, and then began breathing deeply.
It took a while, but I finally stood up and went to
the restroom to collect myself. I decided I needed to
step outside for a moment. I felt claustrophobic.*

*It was terrifying. I thought I was dying.*

*I'm worried. I can't be having episodes like
this. I'm scared I won't be able to function.*

*What's happening to me?*

Yes, that sounds like a panic attack. As you said, such attacks
are terrifying.

When we lose a spouse, our hearts are stunned, and our anxiety
level naturally goes up. Emotion takes over. We become hyperaware of almost everything. Over time, the grief and anxiety
can build to a point where a panic attack occurs.

Most people who have a panic attack almost immediately begin to fear the next one. Of course, that doesn't help matters any.

Don't try to fight the anxiety or keep the panic from coming. This only focuses your mind even more on the anxiety itself. Instead, try to view the panic attack as a release of all your pent-up anxiety, worry, fear, and grief.

If you feel a panic attack coming, breathe. Breathe slowly and deeply—in through the nose and out through the mouth. This is the quickest, easiest, and most effective thing you can do. You can let the panic pass on through rather than holding on to it and letting it take over.

As you breathe deeply, try saying, "Lord, I know you're in this with me. I'm anxious. I'll breathe, and let you handle this."

Be kind to yourself. Be patient with yourself. You've lost your love and life partner. This is hard.

---

*Do not be anxious about anything, but pray about everything, making your requests to God with thanksgiving. And then the peace of God, which is beyond all understanding, will guard your hearts and minds in Christ Jesus.*
*Philippians 4:5-6*

*Lord, You are my peace. I release my anxious thoughts to You. You will lead me through this valley. You are my constant companion.*

# 42

*I think I'm doing a little better, and then I'm
not. It seems like I'm making tiny bits of progress,
then I wonder if I've made any progress at all.
Two steps forward. Three steps back.*

*I have a few moments when the pain recedes into the
background. The next moment, I'm non-functional.
My emotions are volatile and unpredictable.*

*This is discouraging. I feel like I'm constantly
swimming upstream and against the current.
Daily life takes so much more energy now.*

*And I'm doing this alone. I'm
responsible for everything now.*

*My resiliency is gone. I'm not bouncing
back. I'm exhausted.*

It's hard to measure progress in grief after the loss of a spouse.
Grief is not a straight road, but rather more like a winding
path strewn with rocks, holes, twigs, and the occasional log. At
times, you can't see the path at all.

You're in uncharted territory. Feeling lost is natural because
you don't really know where you are. You know what life was,
but not what it is and will be. You're adjusting to what hap-

pened— to the loss of your life partner. This grief journey is arduous and takes time.

You can feel like you're on a treadmill going nowhere. However, if you're trusting the Lord as best you can and processing your grief in healthy ways, you're slowly healing, no matter how it might seem.

Life can only be lived one moment at a time. The grief path can only be walked one step at a time.

Immerse yourself in God's word. Listen as you read. Hear the voice of your shepherd. He is here. He is at work. He is working for you, in you.

---

*Surely your goodness and love will follow me all the days of my life, and I will dwell in the house of the Lord forever.*
*Psalm 23:6*

*Lord, my world is upside down. You, however, have not changed. Your goodness and love follow me everywhere. Cause me to trust You.*

# 43

*There are some mean people out there. They might sound nice and seem helpful, but in the end, they're mean.*

*They don't see or hear me. They judge. They evaluate. Apparently, I don't measure up. They tell me how to fix myself, because I'm the problem. Then they walk away and don't lift a finger to help.*

*Yes, I'm angry today. I'm a bit jaded about humanity. I'm growing more reluctant to trust anyone. My heart can't handle any more beatings.*

*What gives them the right to say these things? Who do they think they are? I've lost my spouse!*

*I know. Breathe. I need to breathe.*

———◆———

You're right. We meet different kinds of people in grief. Sounds like you've been exposed to some hyper-critical judges.

They evaluate others, but not themselves. They push their own issues off on others, hiding behind their platitudes. They are fixers and unsolicited advice-givers. They deliver their edicts and then disappear, only to reappear later to check how well you're following what they told you to do. In order to keep their own struggles at bay, they point out yours.

I've had plenty of experience with these folks too. Most grieving spouses have. Toxic judges are not friends of your heart.

Avoid them. If you can't avoid them, guard your heart and limit their influence. Far from helpful, these people are destructive. Love them and yourself by limiting your exposure to them.

As the hyper-critical judges spout their edicts, see the Lord with you in that moment. Hear Him whisper, "I love you." Far from tossing you platitudes, He enters your grief and walks with you there.

Breathe deeply. Know that He is with you, in you. He invites you to rest in Him.

---

*But you, Lord, do not be far from me. You are my strength; come quickly to help me.*
*Psalm 22:19*

*God, lead me to helpful, supportive people. Enable me to forgive offenses quickly, so that the critical judgments of others do not rule my heart. Work through me, Lord.*

# 44

*I feel so sad.*

*My sadness is a cloud that surrounds me. Some days everything seems sad. All of life is colored by my loss.*

*I miss my spouse. I miss their voice, their presence, and their touch. On days like this, I miss everything.*

*Part of the sadness feels good because it feels right. I should be sad. Then part of me feels guilty. I should be happy for my mate. I should be rejoicing that they are with the Lord and more alive than ever before.*

*Sigh. Sadness can be so heavy. I'm seeing everything through sad lenses.*

———◆———

Sadness is natural, appropriate, and healthy. Your spouse, your love, is gone from your sight. Your heart aches. You love them and want to be with them.

God made us for relationship. Separation, even temporary separation, is painful. Sadness is a natural result.

Pour your sadness out before the Lord. Express your heart to Him. He is the best listener in the universe. He knows all about sadness. He sits with you in this heavy cloud of grief.

Breathe. Openly acknowledge the sadness. Embrace it. Your heart is expressing your love for your mate.

*You are my refuge and my shield; I
have put my hope in your word.
Psalm 119:114*

*Lord, You feel my sadness. I live in You, my
refuge. You are my hope and my life.*

# 45

*Though time has passed, I'm back to
having trouble fathoming all this.*

*How can my love, my soulmate, be gone?*

*I guess my mind doesn't want to accept it. My
heart is having trouble too. I want them back.*

*I want them here—now. I want to see their smile,
hear their voice, and experience their presence.*

*Weird. It's like I woke up one day in another world
-- an alternate universe – and I've been living there
ever since. Enough of this! I want my old life back!*

*Part of me keeps expecting to wake up and
discover this was all a bad dream.*

---

God created us in His image and made us for relationship—with Him and with other people. When physical ties are severed, especially when that tie is our spouse, our hearts shake.

Our minds scream, "No!" Something about it seems wrong. Life feels weird. Surreal. When our life partner is missing from our lives, everything feels off and strange.

Love doesn't disappear. It endures. It lasts. It runs deep and reaches past this life. You love your spouse. Your heart longs to express your love. This is natural and healthy.

Find ways to express your love for your mate. Write a letter. Journal. Draw. Express your affection.

Be honest with God in all this. Share with Him how you long to be with your spouse again. He knows, but He delights in hearing the voice of your heart. He loves you.

---

*When I said, "My foot is slipping," your unfailing love, Lord, supported me.*
*Psalm 94:18*

*God, my world has changed, but you have not.*
*Guide me to grieve well and to express my love.*

# 46

*I'm trying to focus on using my sadness to express my love for my spouse and to thank God for them. I'm giving myself permission to be sad but using it for good. It feels good, and right.*

*Love. Yes, it's about love. I want to keep expressing my love for them and find more ways to do that.*

*Somehow, I think that might help with the sting of missing them. I will always miss them. That's okay. It's about love.*

*My grief proclaims my love, doesn't it?*

---

Yes, it does. You love, and so you grieve. Using your grief to express love for your spouse is wonderful and healing.

Yes, it's about love. And yes, you will always miss them. How could you not? That's natural, and healthy.

Be creative and find more ways to express your love for your partner. When you do, you're also expressing love for God who created them. You can even turn that around and focus on expressing love for Him by grieving well and honoring your loved one.

When we use our grief to fuel gratitude, good things happen.

Our hearts heal. Our souls begin to settle. Love is expressed, and God is honored.

———◆———

*She died at Kiriath Arba that is, Hebron in the land of Canaan, and Abraham went to mourn for Sarah and to weep over her.*
*Genesis 23:2*

*My grief has purpose. I am expressing love. Lord, You are love. You live in me. Help me to do this well.*

# 47

*I've decided to focus on gratitude today.*

*The loss of my spouse is incredibly painful,
but that doesn't mean I can't be thankful.*

*I'm thankful for my spouse. I thank God that
He planned and created them. They were one
of a kind, unique. God did that. He placed
us in each other's lives. He made us one.*

*God did so much for us and through us while we
were together. He gave us wonderful seasons together,
and also led us through extremely difficult periods.*

*I have lost much, but I have much to be
thankful for. I didn't engineer any of that.
It was all given to me. I am blessed.*

*Questions still swirl around inside me, but
for today I will focus on being thankful
for what I had and what I have.*

---

Gratitude is a powerful healing force. It turns the tables on depression and gives our hearts perspective.

God tells us to set our minds on the things above. We are told to fix our thoughts on Jesus. Gratitude is a huge part of this.

Thankfulness comforts the heart. When we choose to take off the glasses of loss and replace them with the lenses of gratitude, our outlook changes. We see more of the bigger picture.

Thankfulness is a wonderful way to honor God and love those who are no longer here. God delights in your thankfulness. He created you. He loves you perfectly.

———◆———

*Rejoice always. Pray continu-*
*ally. Give thanks in everything, for this*
*is God's will for you in Christ Jesus.*
*1 Thessalonians 5:16-18*

*Lord, thank you. You have blessed me in*
*extraordinary ways. Fill me with thankfulness.*

# 48

*I've discovered that some believers will
be supportive, but others aren't.*

*I naturally expected people at church to understand, but
perhaps that was unrealistic. Until I experienced this
terrible loss myself, I didn't have a clue. I was less than
compassionate and supportive to those who were grieving.*

*When someone says something unhelpful, I
try to be patient, but my initial reactions are
powerful. Emotion surges up in me so quickly.
I have to tell myself, "Be quiet. Breathe."*

*I walk away hurt. I feel unseen, belittled,
and more alone. I want to talk about my
spouse. Can't people understand that?*

Of course, you want to talk about your spouse. You love them.
They're priceless and special. Your heart is overflowing with
both grief and gratitude.

And you're right again. People who haven't been through this
deep, soul-wrenching loss can't relate. They might sympathize
for a little while, but they can't empathize.

At first, we naturally expect other believers to be kind, supportive, and understanding, but they will not always be so. Our hearts are eager to share. We want to be able to trust.

Your heart is vulnerable right now, and whom you choose to trust is more important than ever. You need wisdom from the Lord about this. Keep asking the Lord for those safe, trustworthy people. Keep sharing openly and honestly with Him. He will always welcome you. He is always listening.

---

*Be quick to listen, slow to speak,
and slow to become angry.*
***James 1:19***

*Lord, make me loving, patient, and accepting, even in the face of unhelpful, judgmental comments. Love the speaker through me. I will forgive and release quickly.*

# 49

*My kids are starting to look at me funny.*
*They ask why I'm so sad sometimes.*

*I try to shield them from my feelings. I don't want*
*them worrying about me. I don't want to be a*
*dark cloud on their day. So I hide. I fake it.*

*Somehow, that bothers me. I feel like I'm lying to my*
*kids. I feel like they ought to get the real me and not*
*some mask I hand them. After all, they're grieving too.*

*I don't know what to do with this. I feel deceptive and*
*inconsistent. Yet, I know they can handle only so much.*

---

Parenting is hard, period. It's not for sissies. It takes great faith and courage. And now, you're parenting without your spouse, on your own.

Your kids know you're grieving. Treat grieving like you would anything else. Be honest with them, according to their age and ability to understand.

As you said, they're also grieving. Perhaps they're trying to take care of you by masking their grief. Seeing you grieve in healthy ways is a blessing for them. You are modeling for them how to face terrible loss, death, and emotional pain.

It's not about being perfect or getting this right. As long as you're real, authentic, and loving, I don't see how you can lose. Let your heart show a little. Your kids need that. They love you. God is using you to train them to walk with Him through tough times.

Your heavenly Father is good. He is faithful. He will guide you.

———————

*Train children in the way they should go, and when they are old, they will not depart from it.*
**Proverbs 22:6**

*God, You are the ultimate parent. Love, teach, and lead my kids – and use me in this. Let me live before them with honesty and integrity.*

# 50

*I find myself asking uncomfortable questions.*

*Did God take my spouse from me? If God
didn't take them, why did God allow this?
Why didn't He just heal them instead?*

*Couldn't we have had more time?
Why then? Why that way?*

*Today, I can't see any good in what happened.
If that's true, then is God really good?*

*I'm scared to even entertain these thoughts.
I feel ashamed. Yet, my heart keeps
coming back around to them.*

*I have questions. And if I allow myself to think
about it, more questions surface. Ugh.*

---

Loss generates questions, especially the loss of a spouse. This is natural, common, and healthy.

Silencing our hearts by shoving uncomfortable questions aside is not the answer. The questions remain, and seeds of debilitating doubt, anger, and bitterness can begin to grow.

God is not threatened by your questions. He knows your heart.

He knows all your questions already. He invites you to express them honestly to Him.

Consider writing your questions down. See them on the page in front of you. Present them to the Lord. And keep expressing them. He loves you. He is listening.

---

*Why, Lord, do you stand far off? Why do you hide yourself in times of trouble?*
*Psalm 10:1*

*God, I give my questions to You, one by one. Teach me. I trust that You will make clear what You wish to, over time.*

# 51

*I am trying to be honest with God about
the questions roaming in my heart.*

*I've written them down and laid them before Him.
There was something about seeing them on the page that
humbled me. I realized that these questions are natural.*

*My heart wants answers. I want to know why. Even as
I say that, I know that God isn't obligated to explain
all this. I know there are other questions I will never
know the answers to until I'm in heaven. And then,
perhaps all my questions will simply evaporate.*

*I don't know what else to do, so I'll keep sharing
with God what's in my heart. After all, He
already knows my every thought and feeling.*

*My heart aches. I miss my spouse.*

---

We long to understand, yet we know this life is a walk of faith. Faith calls for us to trust amid all kinds of uncertainty.

In the end, I'm not sure there would be many emotionally satisfying answers to our questions at this point. Yet, we must ask. Our hearts are shaking and need reassurance.

When you find yourself wondering why, ask the question, and then return to what you know to be true. God welcomes questions. None of us ever trusts Him 100%. Our faith is mixed with fear, doubt, and wondering.

Jesus meets you where you are, as you are, and loves you there. He will guide you in this. He is good. His love endures forever.

---

*"'If you can'?" said Jesus. "Everything is possible for one who believes." Immediately the boy's father exclaimed, "I do believe; help me overcome my unbelief!"*
*Mark 9:23-24*

*Lord, I trust You. Deepen my trust. You know my questions. More than wanting answers, I want to know You.*

# 52

*I want to share my grief, my questions, and my struggles
with others. I want their input and feedback. Sadly,
most of the time I get blank stares and platitudes.*

*I'm talking about people of faith too. I share a
little and then get those phrases we've all heard a
thousand times with God mixed into them.*

*Some quote Scripture to me. I feel like they're saying, "I
don't have time for this. Here's a spiritual band-aid."*

*I know they mean well. At least, I think they do. Perhaps
it's unfair of me to share and involve them in my grief.*

*But they look concerned and ask how I am. I
share and walk away hurt and disappointed.*

*When animals get hurt, they withdraw.
I understand that now.*

---

Well-meaning people can say some unhelpful things. They
don't know what to do with grief, so they throw a few words at
it and then walk away.

It would be easier if they told us, "I'm concerned about you,
but I don't want you to be sad in my presence or share how
you're feeling." Instead, they try to be nice. Grieving hearts
are left feeling disappointed, alone, and socially unacceptable.

Worse yet, we can begin to feel that something's wrong with us.

Your heart is worth guarding. Try giving brief but honest answers to the questions of others. If they want to know more, they'll ask. Release and forgive those who offend you—and quickly. Your heart doesn't need extra weights right now.

Keep asking God for wisdom. He lives in you. He will teach and guide you in this.

---

*My relatives have gone away; my closest friends have forgotten me.*
*Job 19:14*

*People often don't understand, but You do. I release my frustration, pain, and anger to You, Lord. Lift my heart.*

# 53

*My adult kids are checking on me with concerned
voices and strange looks. I can bet they're thinking
something like, "Move on. Pull out of this."*

*I know they love me. They want me to feel better.
Watching me grieve is hard for them. Perhaps their
grief is driving them to push me to be okay.*

*Are they grieving? They don't seem to be showing it.
Honestly, I'm angry with how they're behaving.*

*I am where I am. I feel what I feel.
I'm doing the best I can.*

*Some encouragement and understanding
instead of, "You need to move on," would
be nice. Why can't we grieve together?*

*What do I do with this? I usually hide a little more.
I fake it, but my heart is squirming inside.*

---

It's hard for adult children to watch their parents hurt – especially if it's their one remaining parent. They're desperately trying to protect what they have left. They want us to be happy,
content, and problem-free.

We humans have a hard time with grief. We can't seem to be
quiet and respectful in the presence of sadness or emotional

suffering. We try to relieve our own pain by directing the grief process of someone else. We judge, try to fix the unfixable, or run.

Grief scares us. We don't know what to do with it.

Seek the Lord about this. Pour out your concerns to Him. He knows how challenging parenting can be. He is very familiar with His children not understanding Him. His children try to tell Him what to do all the time too.

Pray for ways to be honest and yet protect your own heart too. The Lord will give you wisdom. He understands. His love for you is perfect.

---

*If any of you lacks wisdom, you should ask God, who gives generously to all without finding fault, and it will be given to you.*
*James 1:5*

*Lord, give me faith to accept where my kids are right now. Express your love through me to my children. Be their comfort, and mine.*

# 54

*I'm having headaches lately. And stomach distress.*
*I'm tired all the time. I'm not sleeping well.*

*It feels like I'm always on the verge of getting*
*sick. Is grief taking its toll on my body too?*

*I move through the days with less energy. I*
*feel like I'm just going through the motions.*
*I feel frustrated and confused.*

*From the moment my spouse died, I started to*
*disappear. I feel like a shadow of my former*
*self. Now, even my body is betraying me.*

———◆———

When we lose a life partner, grief hits our entire being. It affects us emotionally, mentally, spiritually, and physically.

Grief is a form of stress. Over time, it can suppress our immune systems. We can begin having all sorts of physical symptoms—headaches, stomach distress, palpitations, panic attacks, raised blood pressure, aches and pains, etc.

We're wired for relationship. Death and separation create great stress. Our hearts wrestle with this deeply personal loss. Our minds try desperately to make sense of things.

No wonder you feel as you do. If you're concerned about your health, please see a physician. Make sure you tell them about the traumatic loss you're enduring.

Breathe deeply. Take your health seriously. Downgrade your expectations. Rest in the Lord. God can handle this. Release burdens and fears to Him. Seek to do only what He puts on your plate today.

--------

*"Be merciful to me, Lord, for I am in distress; my eyes grow weak with sorrow, my soul and body with grief."*
**Psalm 31:9**

*Lord, You know what's happening inside me. Heal me. Give me wisdom to know what to do. You are my peace.*

# 55

*I've said before that I felt like I wasn't really living but
just going through the motions. I feel foggy. Tired. Numb.*

*Numb. That's it. I'm one big ball of
emotion, but I can't seem to feel it.*

*I look around and watch the world speeding
along. I'm a part of it, but I can't seem to
enter in. My spouse is gone. My old life has
disappeared. I'm dazed. Stunned. Fatigued.*

*I sit and stare at the walls. I drive and forget where
I'm going. I have conversations, but I'm not all there.*

*I don't like this. Is my heart shutting down?*

———◆———

There comes a time in our grief process where most of us feel
numb. Our hearts have been trying to manage all the emotions
swirling around in us. Our minds have been active, desperately
working through what has happened and all that it means.
Perhaps our souls have been shaken.

The loss of our spouse has upended everything. No wonder
we're dazed, sad, angry, anxious, fatigued, confused, and
depressed.

At some point, our system needs a break. Our feelers shut
down. Our minds go on autopilot. We begin to function on

energy-save mode. Feeling numb is common and natural in grief. Usually, it's a temporary rest stop on our grief journey.

Breathe. Accept yourself where you are. The Lord is at work in you and for you. As much as possible, let Him carry you. Now is not forever. Your grief will change over time.

*My heart is broken within me; all my bones tremble.*
*Jeremiah 23:9*

*Lord, You are my life. My hope is in You. Support me now. Hold me up. Remind me of your love.*

# 56

*I'm beyond sadness. I feel depressed.*

*The color has gone out of my life.*

*Nothing looks good, sounds good, or tastes good. I lie in bed in the morning and don't want to get up. I drag myself through the day. I put up my facade and focus on getting through the time without drawing too much attention or embarrassing myself too badly.*

*My heart is exhausted. I'm a shell. I feel empty.*

*The loneliness is exhausting.*

———◆———

Grief is truly exhausting. It takes enormous energy.

Your spouse is gone. Your life has been upended, perhaps even shattered. All the change is overwhelming.

Change is demanding, stressful, and incredibly exhausting—especially change we don't like or didn't want.

Most grieving hearts experience some depression. As believers in Christ, we tend to hide this. We're embarrassed, even ashamed. We feel like we've failed. We tell ourselves that we are people of faith and should be stronger than this.

Job, Hannah, Naomi, David, Elijah, Jeremiah, and other biblical characters wrestled with depression at times. You're in good company. You're human. You're finite and limited.

Be honest with God about all this. He knows already. He loves you. He wants to hear your voice expressing your heart to Him. Even now, He is at work in you.

———◆———

*You who are my Comforter in sorrow, my heart is faint within me.*
*Jeremiah 8:18*

*Lord, You are my Comforter. I lay my numb heart in your hands. Work in me. Restore me. You are my hope.*

# 57

*I feel better today, and I know why.*

*A coworker asked me to lunch. While we were waiting for our food, they asked me how I was doing and added, "Yes, I really want to know."*

*I blinked. I started talking. I stopped at points and looked them in the eye. They were still listening. I talked on and on.*

*The food came, and I kept talking. Words poured out of me like water.*

*When we arrived back at work, I felt lighter—like someone had pushed a button and released some pressure. It felt good.*

---

Part of being created in the image of God and designed for relationship is that all of us long to be seen and heard. When we're grieving, this becomes even more important.

Your coworker saw you. They listened. They heard not only your words, but your heart. They didn't evaluate you or attempt to fix you. You were able to share and to grieve, freely and safely. No wonder you felt better.

Thank God for His provision. He puts the people around us

people that we need. He expresses His goodness and His love through them. He is at work for us, for you, all the time.

I rejoice with you. Safe people are a true gift from God.

———❖———

*Now that you have purified yourselves by obeying the truth so that you have sincere love for each other, love one another deeply, from the heart.*
*1 Peter 1:22*

*Lord, put people in my life who are safe and loving. Lead me to them. You know my needs. I trust You.*

# 58

*Being listened to and heard felt so good,*
*I decided to return the favor.*

*I contacted a friend whom I knew might be struggling.*
*I let them talk. Before we ended the call, they told*
*me how much the conversation had meant to them.*

*All I did was listen. Listening is powerful. I*
*wish I had done more of it in the past.*

*I resolve to be a better listener in the future.*
*I was able to give something. I believe I*
*made a difference. That felt good.*

*I feel hopeful. If I can serve others while enduring*
*this terrible loss, perhaps that will help me heal.*

---

Listening is powerful indeed.

Our world is noisy. Everyone seems busy beyond belief. We race frantically through our days, checking off items on our mental to-do lists. We rarely take time to listen. We all end up missing out.

We all have hearts. We've all been wounded. We all need relationships. We all need to be heard. Listening is one of life's greatest skills.

The Lord is always listening. He knows you and hears your heart. He is the ultimate listener.

When we listen, we reflect Him. We meet people where they are, as they are, and love them. When we feel heard, we heal a little. No wonder it felt good.

Listening well and without judgment is one way you can honor your spouse and love those around you.

———◆———

*Then Jesus said, "Whoever*
*has ears to hear, let them hear".*
*Mark 4:9*

*Lord, give me a listening heart. Let me*
*hear your voice. Let me hear the hearts of*
*others. Work in and through me.*

# 59

*Work continues to be a challenge.*

*I've fallen into a rhythm of steeling myself
to be fake, survive the day, and grieve in
little bits here and there when I can.*

*Honestly, work is a welcome distraction at times.
It gives my mind somewhere to go. I wish I
could focus more. I still blip out at times.*

*I try not to think about the next grief burst—when,
where, what I'm going to do, etc. I can easily walk
around cringing, waiting for the ceiling to fall. I
refuse to do that. I don't want to live that way.*

*My heart isn't in my work. I'm just
going through the motions.*

*The emptiness inside me feels massive. I wish things
were different. I wish I had my spouse back.*

---

Much of your heart is taken up with grief at present. There's less of you available for work. Because your life has changed, your work is different too.

Distractions can be healthy. Our hearts can't handle the intensity of spousal grief 24-7. Zoning out is natural and even healthy. Your heart and mind are taking a much-needed break.

Grief bursts will come but focusing on them only leads to anxiety and fear. God is with you. He can handle it. You will get through it. Grief bursts are essentially pressure releases for your heart. You're expressing love for one who is no longer here. You're feeling their absence.

Your work performance won't be at the usual level right now—and that's okay. You're missing your spouse. Give yourself a lot of mercy and grace.

God is at work in and through you. Accept yourself. Receive His love for you. Look for His gifts today.

*I pray that out of His glorious riches he may strengthen you with power through His Spirit in your inner being, so that Christ may dwell in your hearts through faith.*
**Ephesians 3:16-17**

*God, You can handle all things. I release myself and all things to You. Strengthen me.*

# 60

*I'm feeling guilty again.*

*I find myself thinking about what I could
have done or should have said. All the unkind
words and actions toward my spouse flood my
mind and threaten to drown me at times.*

*I know I'm not perfect, but I wish I could have
been more patient and loving at those times. I keep
wondering if I caused this somehow. Am I responsible?*

*Sometimes I think, "Yes, it's my fault."
That's devastating. I can't stay there long,
or I end up in a very dark place.*

*Guilt is like a boomerang. It keeps coming back.
It circles back around, over and over again.*

---

When we lose a spouse, it's natural to look back and remember. When we do, we see regrets as well as joys. Regrets often morph into guilt.

Regret says, "I wish it could have been different, and I wish I had this-or-that." Guilt says, "It's all my fault, and I'm responsible." Regrets must simply be accepted as such over time. We don't hold ourselves hostage over them. Guilt, however, is poison to the heart.

The antidote for guilt is forgiveness. Jesus died for all our sins – past, present, and future. Receiving His forgiveness sets us free from guilt's persistent accusations.

Share your regrets with the Lord. Present your heart and anything you feel guilty about to Him. Lay your "what-if's" and "if-only's" before Him.

Watch His face. See His love and acceptance. Embrace His total forgiveness.

Whenever guilt comes knocking, forgive yourself again. Release. Let the guilt pass on through.

———◆———

*But with you there is forgiveness, so that
we can, with reverence, serve you.*
**Psalm 130:4**

*Lord, here is my heart. Your forgiveness is
perfect. I rest in what Christ did for me.
I receive your acceptance and love.*

# 61

*What do I do with my spouse's things?*

*I've been putting off even asking that question. I don't want to deal with this.*

*At first, I thought I would keep everything forever. Then I thought I might give everything away. Now, I don't know. I can't leave things as they are, can I?*

*Reminders of my love are everywhere. Every possession seems packed with memories. Right now, most of those memories bring pain. Will it always be this way?*

*I know dealing with my partner's things is part of this whole process, but I don't know what I should do or how.*

---

Dealing with a spouse's belongings is a difficult, painful part of the grief process. There is no right way or perfect timing to do this. Every widowed spouse's grief journey is unique.

Some deal with their partner's possessions quickly, while others take years. Most tackle this challenge in stages, deciding over time what they want to keep and what they want to give away.

Our spouse's belongings are special because they are what we have left. They represent the person, and our hearts are reluctant to say goodbye and let go.

The Lord feels your pain and knows your heart. Ask Him for

guidance. What would be most loving toward Him, yourself, and your loved one?

Take your time. Let your heart be guided by love.

---

*Peter went with them, and when he arrived, he was taken upstairs to the room. All the widows stood around him, crying and showing him the robes and other clothing that Dorcas had made while she was still with them.*
*Acts 9:39*

*Lord, reminders of my spouse are everywhere. I don't know what to do, how, or when. Guide me. I will rest in You and trust that You will lead me.*

# 62

*I decided to go through my spouse's
things a little bit at a time.*

*Surprisingly, some items are easy to deal with. Other
things, however, I put right back in the drawer or
box. I guess I'm not ready to decide about those yet.*

*I'm amazed how things can carry a person's
presence. Most of my mate's possessions have
memories attached to them. My emotions surge up
and bounce all over the place. This is hard.*

*I tell myself it's just a bunch of stuff, but my
heart is not getting the message. This is going to
take more time and energy than I thought.*

*I guess I need to either push through
or adjust my expectations.*

After the death of a spouse, we tend to cling tightly to what
we have left. Possessions are attached to people. Some things
become infinitely precious after a loss.

For most of us, dealing with a spouse's possessions is an emotional roller coaster. Drawers, closets, boxes, and rooms are
stuffed with potential grief triggers. We see something, and the
memories come flooding in. We touch something else, and our

hearts mourn. Thankfully, the same basic grief truths apply to possessions.

God is with you and in you. Be real with Him and share continually. Be patient and loving toward yourself. Take your time.

The goal is not to deal with your partner's possessions. The goal is intimacy with God amid the pain and confusion.

Grief is not a checklist, but a journey of the heart.

---

*Because you are my help, I sing in the shadow of your wings. I cling to you; your right hand upholds me.*
**Psalm 63:7-8**

*I cling to You, Lord. This widowed walk is about intimacy with You. I will focus on You and trust that You will make all things clear in time.*

# 63

*My emotions are stirred up from dealing with my
love's possessions—or trying to. I feel agitated, sad,
and lost. My grief feels extra heavy at present.*

*I feel like I'm going backwards. I seem to
be reliving so much lately. Memories swirl
around me. I feel dizzy sometimes.*

*The more emotional I am, the more challenging work
and relationships become. Grief makes everything harder.*

*When I'm more of a mess, I want to
withdraw. I pull back and start protecting
myself more. I've had enough pain.*

*I've been at this grief thing for a bit, but I still feel lost
and alone. I feel overwhelmed and shaky right now.*

———

Grief is always moving. Like any journey, some portions will
be harder and more demanding than others.

On this widowed walk, so much is painful, sad, and frustrating. Some parts of your grief path will be especially rocky,
uphill, and challenging.

You can only take one step at a time and live one moment at a
time. The task is learning to navigate what's in front of you in a

sane and healthy way, while trying not to jump ahead. As you process it, your grief will change over time.

Grief is unpredictable, and we never know what's coming next. But we do know God. He is constant. He never changes. He is forever the same. He is love.

As much as possible, be authentic with Him. Share honestly with Him about what's happening inside you. Yes, He already knows, but He wants to hear it from you. He loves the voice of your heart.

***

*Jesus Christ is the same yesterday and today and forever.*
*Hebrews 13:8*

*Everything seems to be changing. You, Lord, never change. I rest in You. You are my constant, faithful companion on this rocky road.*

# 64

*I don't feel like me anymore. And it's getting worse.*

*I miss my love, my spouse. I miss our
life. I miss me. I miss us.*

*I find myself wondering who I am now. I wonder if
I'm going to make it through this. If I do, I wonder
what I'll be like on the other side of this grief.*

*I used to know these answers, but now I'm
wondering about a lot. I'm in some in-between
place that seems uncertain and foggy.*

*I feel like I'm drifting, but don't know where.*

---

The loss of a spouse tends to throw most of us into a sort of identity crisis. Since we're designed by God for relationship, death can deal a stunning blow to our sense of who we are.

In an instant, with our life partner's final breath, we find ourselves in another world. Our life has been altered. Everything takes on a different hue and shade. Loss hits the heart, and therefore affects everything.

We find ourselves in the valley of the shadow of death that King David talks about in Psalm 23. We're no longer in green pastures or beside still waters. We're in an unfamiliar and foreboding place. It can feel dark and scary.

Psalm 23 reminds us that journeying through such places is part of this life. But it is also a valley that we emerge from. It might be hard to grasp, but the implication is that there is more green grass and still water on the other side of this season of grief.

God is leading you through this territory. Through is the key word. Now is not forever.

Be kind to yourself. Rest in God's kindness, goodness, and love. He will guide you.

---

*Even though I walk through the darkest valley, I will fear no evil, for you are with me; your rod and your staff, they comfort me.*
**Psalm 23:4**

*You walk with me, Lord. You lead me. You are my constant companion. I am yours. I will trust You and take one step at a time.*

# 65

*I know there is good all around me. I can
see it. In my family. In people. In life.*

*At the same time, I can't seem to feel the good
that's there. I'm surrounded with love, but I
can't embrace it. Lately, I feel nothing.*

*My spouse is no longer here. My heart is crushed.
My emotions have exhausted me. I don't think
I have any feelings left. I'm empty. Tired.*

*And then I think of all my responsibilities.
Everything falls to me now.*

*I want to hide.*

---

You're grappling with the death of your spouse, your life partner. Your heart is exhausted with grief. It's taking a break, trying to recover. Yes, there is good all around you. You will appreciate and feel all the good again, but perhaps not right now.

This is frustrating. We can feel disconnected and not part of the world around us. We're dazed. We're exhausted and numb.

I think of the final verse in Psalm 23. This was King David's summation of life. "Surely goodness and love will follow me all the days of my life, and I will dwell in the house of the Lord forever." We need not chase love and goodness. Love and goodness are all around us. God surrounds us with them. Goodness and love accompany and follow us wherever we go.

I guess that's not surprising. God is love. He is goodness. He is with you. He walks with you.

Breathe. Rest in Him.

---

*Surely your goodness and love will follow me all the days of my life, and I will dwell in the house of the Lord forever.*
**Psalm 23:6**

*Though many times I don't feel it, I trust that I am surrounded by your love and goodness, Lord. Give me eyes to see You. Let me experience your love more than ever.*

# 66

*I used to wake up in the morning and look forward
to the day. I expected good things. I had joy.*

*Now I open my eyes and lie there, deeply aware of
my spouse's absence. I force myself to get moving.
Everything seems to take much more mental energy.*

*I don't feel depressed. At least I don't think so.
I feel sluggish, like I'm not all there. It's as if I
have half a heart. Part of me is missing.*

*My motivation is waning. My sense of
purpose has almost disappeared.*

*I feel like a shadow.*

———◆———

Grief can take its toll over time. The heaviness of our loss
weighs us down. Routine life takes more conscious effort and
energy.

Since we're created by God for relationship, when someone as
close as a spouse dies, our hearts are shaken, broken, and even
shattered. At first, we're stunned. As life continues, we feel the
pain. We keep walking forward, but with a pronounced limp.

Your life partner is missing. You feel this intensely. Your heart
knows. Life is different. You are different.

The Lord is your strength, your energy, your life. He holds

your heart. He heals you as you are real with Him about what's happening inside you.

This is a season of deep grief, and the Lord is guiding you through it. He is good. He is faithful. He is love.

———◆———

*I love you, Lord, my strength.*
*Psalm 18:1*

*Lord, I have no strength apart from You. My heart is broken. Be merciful to me and heal me. You are my light and my hope.*

# 67

*Will things ever feel good again? Will I*
*have joy again? Is it okay to have joy?*

*I feel like I should be sad, but I don't like it.*
*When I do smile, I feel guilty later. My mind*
*is saying it's wrong to have anything good right*
*now. It's as if joy would be disrespectful.*

*I feel caught. Stuck. I don't know if I'm the one making*
*these decisions, or whether grief is driving me along.*

*I don't feel in charge of my life, my emotions, or*
*anything. I'm at the whim of events, other people's words*
*and reactions, and my own unpredictable emotions.*

*I'm in this gloomy room called widowed*
*grief and I can't seem to get out.*

---

God is gracious. He gives relief amid pain. He gives joy and delight to grieving hearts. He shines light in dark places.

Your spouse would not deny you joy. They would not wish guilt and pain upon you. If they could, they would shower you with peace, healing, and contentment.

Now is a season of grief, but it is not a time bereft of hope and joy. Hope and joy are always here, but perhaps you don't feel them the way you're used to.

It can feel like you're being swept along by a river of grief, stuck in its strong, swift current. In reality, you're on an unknown path, walking with the Lord, taking one step at a time.

Take your emotions seriously. Feel them. Be honest with God about them today. He is your light. He is with you in your darkest places. He embraces your grieving heart.

*Very truly I tell you, you will weep and mourn while the world rejoices. You will grieve, but your grief will turn to joy.*
**John 16:20**

*Lord, I accept this season of grief. Now is not forever. I will receive and treasure the joy you give me along the way. You are my light.*

# 68

*I feel limp and lifeless. No stamina. No
motivation. No sense of purpose or direction.
I'm just here, going through the motions.*

*All my energy is focused on getting through
the day, somehow, some way.*

*I don't know how long I can do this. I need
something to change. I don't like this new life.
It's like my heart has departed. Perhaps my
heart is gone. Maybe it left with my spouse.*

*I loved my spouse. I love them still. I never dreamed I
would have to do life without them. I still feel married.*

*I don't know how to do this. I know life
goes on. I know God is with me. I know
all these things, but this still hurts.*

*I feel lost and alone.*

---

In the intense grief from the loss of a spouse, the heart mourns.
We're missing our soulmate, our love, our life partner. We
don't know how to process this. We don't know what to think
or how to feel.

Life becomes not only painful, but confusing. All our energies
become focused on the essentials of life. Moving, working, eat-

ing, sleeping, and fulfilling responsibilities. These things now require herculean effort. There is little to no energy left for anything else.

Our sense of purpose takes a hit. With our spouse gone, we can wonder why we're here. Our motivation seems to evaporate.

God carries us all the time. We never walk, work, or do life on our own. In seasons of grief, we become even more conscious of this. Our fragility and vulnerability show, and we don't like it.

He carries you. He is your life. You were made for relationship with Him. The Lord knows your wounds. He is your Healer.

*When He rose from prayer and went back to the disciples, He found them asleep, exhausted from sorrow.*
*Luke 22:45*

*Lord, grief has exhausted me. You are my hope, my strength, and my life. Heal my wounds. I rest in You. I trust You.*

# 69

*I know I've said this before. I don't feel like me.*
*I miss my old life. I miss my spouse. I miss us.*

*I don't know how to navigate this new, bumpy,*
*and unpredictable terrain. I don't know*
*who I am. I don't know why I'm here. My*
*sense of identity and purpose is gone.*

*What do I do? Do I keep getting up in the*
*morning, hoping that my heart and sense*
*of purpose will return someday?*

*Life seems so dull and gray. My sunshine is gone.*
*Everything seems gloomy. When the sun does peek*
*through, it's almost as if I chase it away.*

---

Grieving spouses wonder about many things. Everything can seem uncertain and up in the air. We can feel lost.

It's as if a sinkhole opened under us and we're in a free fall to who knows where. Fear of the unknown can threaten our hearts. We brace for more loss. Our sense of hope diminishes.

Your world has been altered. With your spouse gone, nothing is quite the same. Your heart has been broken. This affects everything.

Even with all this, your purpose is there, safe and intact. As you walk with the Lord through this valley, He will speak to you. He is your comfort. He is your strength. He is your purpose.

God has not distanced Himself or disappeared. He's in this with you, all the way. Right now, you're in grief recovery. This takes time and loads of energy. God is working in you and through you more than you realize. He is giving to you, even in this season when you feel so empty.

You may not feel these realities. That's okay. Accept yourself. Lean into God. Keep your heart open to Him. Share openly and honestly. He is listening. He knows your heart.

———————

***Look to the Lord and His strength;***
***seek His face always.***
***Psalm 105:4***

*My world is upended. Lord, I look to You.*
*You are my strength. You know all things.*
*Amid the turmoil, I choose to seek You.*

# 70

*I'm single now. What does that mean?*

*I don't want to be single. I'm widowed.
I still see myself as married.*

*I certainly feel married, even though my
spouse is gone and not coming back.*

*Am I single but married at the same time?
Strange. All of this is so strange.*

*People are urging me to move on. "You need
to get out more." "Maybe you need to date."
"I know someone you should meet."*

*Really? I wish they could hear how ridiculous
that sounds to me. My heart is still married.*

---

In our world, single seems to mean "unattached." That's not you. Though widowed, you're still very much attached. Two hearts that become one don't simply become two again.

Widowed spouses tussle with this new, dual identity – married, but widowed. The contradictions of your new life are naturally mentally confusing and emotionally frustrating.

Your heart needs time and space to grieve, heal, and adjust. There are no time limits on this. You are unique. So was your spouse and your partnership. Your grief process will be uniquely your own.

Jesus walks with you in this. He knows this road well. He knows you. He is guiding, teaching, and caring for you right now – and in every moment ahead.

Grief is a process, not a checklist. The Lord knows what is ahead. Try to trust Him with the future. The Lord will show you the way today, one step, one moment at a time.

*I am like a desert owl, like an owl among the ruins. I lie awake; I have become like a bird alone on a roof.*
**Psalm 102:6-7**

*Lord, You know all things. Remind me to walk with You in the present and trust You with the future.*

# 71

*Apparently, my spouse didn't tell me everything.*

*I've found out some things I didn't know. I don't know what to do with this. I don't need any more surprises.*

*I feel betrayed. Did they lie to me? Did they hide this deliberately? Why?*

*I find myself wondering what else I don't know. I thought we shared everything. I was wrong.*

*I certainly didn't expect this. I'm angry and disappointed.*

*What do I do with this?*

---

I'm so sorry. To feel betrayed after a death is awful.

This is terribly painful. Please do what you can to guard your heart in all this. Find healthy ways to express what is happening inside you – the thoughts and emotions. Write it out in a journal. Compose a letter to your spouse. Share with a safe person. Process this new trauma and get it out.

And, as quickly as possible, for the sake of your own heart, forgive. By forgiving, you're saying it mattered and it hurt, but you aren't going to let this control your heart.

Thankfully, nothing is hidden from the Lord. Your experience is a fulfillment of one of His promises – that everything hidden will be revealed.

Process this event well – as much as you need to. Forgiving and releasing this may take time. Be real with the Lord and your own heart.

The Lord is an expert at taking things like this and using it for your good. Lean hard into Him. He knows all about betrayal and people trying to hide things. He grieves over this. He loves you.

---

*For there is nothing hidden that will not be disclosed, and nothing concealed that will not be known or brought out into the open.*
*Luke 18:7*

*Lord, protect my heart. Empower me to accept this and to forgive. Thank you for accepting and forgiving me. Help me to rest in You.*

# 72

*I now understand a little more why people can run to alcohol, drugs, or food. The pain of life can be immense. The fear and worry can drive a person to the brink.*

*I want relief. I've noticed I'm drinking more. It used to be a glass of wine here and there. Now, it's more than a glass, more than occasionally. I don't think I'm an alcoholic, at least not yet.*

*I'm trying to get through this time as sanely as possible. If I'm drinking more, does that mean I'm depressed?*

*I'm caring less and less about things, about myself, and about life.*

---

None of us like pain, especially emotional pain. We don't know what to do with it. We tend to run from it rather than feeling it through. We run to entertainment, food, alcohol, work, shopping, hobbies, collecting, and drugs. If something promises relief and distraction, we lunge for it.

Of course, none of these things satisfy. As grief relief, they don't work. The grief is still there, and the emotional pain boomerangs back with a vengeance. Now we have extra guilt to deal with too.

As we are honest with ourselves, the Lord, and a few other

people about what's going on inside us, some of the pressure is released. We feel through some of the pain and process some of the grief. The need for addictions wanes.

Breathe. See the Lord walking with you in this pain. He longs for you to give yourself to Him so that He can work in and through you and bring comfort, peace, and hope. Lay your heart in His hands. Experience His love today.

*And I pray that you, being rooted and established in love, may have power, together with all the Lord's holy people, to grasp how wide and long and high and deep is the love of Christ, and to know this love that surpasses knowledge—that you may be filled to the measure of all the fullness of God.*
*Ephesians 3:17-19*

*Lord, enable me to experience your perfect love. Surround me with it and immerse me in it. Calm my troubled heart. You are love. You are life.*

# 73

*I know I need safe, trustworthy people in my
life right now. I'm having trouble finding
them. People that I counted on are gone, or at
least most of them. Disappeared. Poof.*

*It's like being widowed is a disease and I'm
contagious. People are avoiding me. I can sense it.*

*I'm angry. Then I laugh. If I were them, I would avoid
me too. Who wants to be around sorrow and pain?*

*I'm alone now, and I feel more isolated by the
day. I can look back and see myself pulling away.
I know this isn't healthy, but my disappointment
with the lack of support has driven me here.*

*I don't know what to do. I need help.*

When we don't know what to do, we back up to what we know
to be true, no matter what.

God is real. He thought of you, wanted you, and planned you
even before He created the earth and the world. He loved you
and loves you still. His love is perfect.

He created you for relationship with Himself and others. He
places people in your life, and you in theirs. We're designed

to love each other and do life together. He has safe people out there for you.

You need some people that know grief and know it well. Some find these people in grief support groups. People who were on the periphery of your life, or perhaps some you didn't know at all, can become major players in your recovery, healing, and growth.

Safe people who know grief will gladly walk with you through this painful, uncharted territory.

Ask God to bring these people into your life. Ask Him to guide you to them. Perhaps you know who they are already. Reach out. Your heart needs support. You are more important than you realize.

---

*But if we walk in the light, as He is in the light, we have fellowship with one another, and the blood of Jesus, His Son, purifies us from all sin.*
*1 John 1:7*

*Lord, open my eyes to recognize the safe people around me. I want heart connection. I need fellowship. Surround me with healing.*

# 74

*Support groups? That sounds scary.*

*I don't think of myself as a timid person, but the
idea of showing up fills me with fear and dread.
I'm already feeling vulnerable and on edge.*

*Does talking about this with other people
help? What if they judge me?*

*What are support groups like anyway? It feels risky.
Part of me says, "No way. I'm going to do this alone.
It's safer that way." But then, I know where that kind
of thinking leads – to greater loneliness and isolation.*

*How do I do this? Where do I go? I'm apprehensive.
Will they take my heart and my pain seriously?*

---

Most grieving spouses are reluctant to try a support group.
It takes courage and resolve to enter a room with people you
don't know when your heart is already shaking.

Healing is a battle. Your heart is under assault. Grief is not the
enemy, but guilt, isolation, bitterness, and self-condemnation
are. It's a spiritual battle. We don't fight these enemies alone.
We need courageous comrades in it with us. There are others
out there – some widowed spouses among them – who are
ready and able to walk with you through this season of grief.

Is there a support group at your church? If not, is there one at a church near you? Perhaps try local hospices. If you can't find a physical group, there are grief support groups available online.

Most of the good and healing things in life are scary and re-quire courage. In this case, it requires faith. God has people out there to walk with you through this. He wants to use you in their lives too.

---

*"Be strong and courageous. Do not be afraid; do not be discouraged, for the Lord your God will be with you wherever you go."*
*Joshua 1:9*

*God, You are my strength. Work in me and move me to places and people of hope and healing. You go before me. Give me courage and faith to follow.*

# 75

*You said God wants to use me in other people's lives? That's a good one. Maybe in the future, if I ever get better, but surely not like I am now.*

*I'm a mess. I'm no good to anyone. My own kids sigh when they see or talk to me. Everyone wants me to get over this, as if death and grief are like the common cold.*

*I'm focused on survival, and I'm not doing well at even that. Every day is like doing water aerobics in the middle of the ocean. No relief. Just more exhaustion.*

*I sound terribly cynical, don't I? I wonder where my faith went. I know it's still there, but it must be hiding somewhere. I certainly don't feel it.*

*I miss my old life. I miss my spouse.*

---

Grief is taking up a lot of space in your life at present. It's demanding and draining. There's less of you left for the rest of life. No wonder you're frustrated.

Even if everyone around you seems to be avoiding you, trying to fix you, and pelting you with platitudes and advice, there are people out there who understand. Your loss and grief are unique, but some understand what it means to be hurt, confused, crushed, or even devastated. Many of them have lost spouses.

These people are out there, and they're waiting for you. They're looking for people like you to walk with them. You don't have to be on the top of your game for God to use you. You just have to be willing.

God can use anyone, anytime, anywhere. You will often be unaware that God is working in and through you. That happens as you trust Him and simply show up.

If trying a support group is still scary, consider asking a friend to go with you the first time. What do you have to lose?

———❖———

*That is why, for Christ's sake, I delight in weaknesses, in insults, in hardships, in persecutions, in difficulties. For when I am weak, then I am strong.*
*2 Corinthians 12:10*

*You are always at work and things are not always as they seem to be. I present myself to You. I believe You live in me. Live through me, Lord.*

# 76

*My mind is not what it used to be.*

*I'm forgetting things—more than usual. I can't seem to think straight. I have trouble finding words when I'm in conversation. I blink and forget what we were talking about.*

*At first, I thought it was just the fatigue. Now, I don't know. I'm worried there might be something wrong with me. I don't feel like myself at all.*

*It feels like my brain isn't working right. Is this grief too?*

*I wish my love was still here. I miss my spouse desperately.*

———◆———

Most likely, yes—it's grief. If you're concerned about your health, however, please get checked out. Sometimes, we need reassurance more than anything.

Grief affects us mentally, especially with the loss of a spouse. Our cognitive functions are not what they used to be. Grief is taking up much of your internal space. Details—like where you put something, appointments, and what you were just talking about—tend to fall through the cognitive cracks.

As you walk with the Lord and move through your grief, the mental fog will begin to clear over time. Those cognitive abilities you miss will most likely bounce back with proper self-care.

The Lord knows your limitations. He is handling many, many things for you, right now. The Lord is patient with you. Be patient with yourself.

God is comforting and ministering to you in your pain and grief. He is healing your heart, though at times you may not feel that way. He is good, and His love for you is perfect.

*But David found strength in the Lord his God.*
*1 Samuel 30:6*

*Lord, You are patient with me. Enable me*
*to be patient with myself. You are my life. I*
*release all worry and concern to You.*

# 77

*I'm still not sleeping well. I wake up
at night. My mind races.*

*I lie there, thinking about my spouse. Their
absence is palpable. The silence is crushing.*

*Everything descends upon me in the
dark. Guilt swirls in my brain.*

*I often wake up sweating and anxious. I still have
dreams, and a few nightmares. I see my love in my mind's
eye in the middle of the night. The sadness is intense.*

*The questions start circling again. I feel
like I'm right back where I started.*

*No matter how much time goes by, my partner's
death seems like yesterday. The feelings are fresh,
all over again, for the hundredth time.*

---

Almost all grieving spouses report that nighttime is difficult.
We lay our heads on the pillow and our minds flow to where
our hearts are -- with our departed mate and life partner. Our
thoughts begin to race, faster and faster. Waking up to an
anxiety attack is not uncommon. Our minds and hearts are
processing our pain and grief, even while we sleep.

As you lie there at night, breathe deeply. Focus on your breathing. See the Lord with you (because He is). Imagine Him speaking to you—comforting and reassuring you.

I believe He is always speaking to us. We need ears to hear Him. Turn your thoughts toward Him. Tune in to His voice. Slow down the thought train and let His word bathe your mind and heart.

God is with you in the night. He is speaking. He is listening. He is loving you, even while you sleep.

———◈———

*If I say, "Surely the darkness will hide me and the light become night around me," even the darkness will not be dark to you; the night will shine like the day, for darkness is as light to you.*
**Psalm 139:11-12**

*Lord, You are my constant companion. You never leave me. Speak to me and bring your comfort in the night. Give me sleep. I rest in You.*

# 78

*I found a support group. I haven't contacted anyone yet, but I know where and when it meets.*

*I'm still nervous about this. My mind says, "Don't bother. It's not going to help. This will be a waste of time and energy." Then I think, "Why not go and try it? What do I have to lose? Yes, this is scary, but I've done plenty of scary things in my life."*

*I wish I knew what it was going to be like. That would help.*

*I feel like I need to be emotionally and mentally prepared to walk in there. I wish I was less fearful – and more courageous.*

*It seems like my courage and confidence departed with my spouse.*

---

Almost every grieving spouse wonders these things about support groups. If there's a contact person or number to call, reach out. Ask them for more information. They'll gladly tell you what the group is like and how it operates. You might even be able to talk to the leader or facilitator.

Reaching out takes energy, but it's well worth it. It's not really about courage, but about faith. Do you believe God will be with you as you go and bless you no matter what? Do you believe He has people there He has prepared for you, and you for them?

It can be difficult, in times of loss, to look for and see the good. We must set our minds on God and His goodness. Our hearts need the reassurance that He is ordering all things for our good. Our minds need the reminder that He has a plan for us—a good plan.

Chew on God's Word. Breathe deeply and take in what He has said. Listen as He speaks to you. When fearful or worried, let your mind go to comforting, uplifting scriptures.

God speaks through what He has spoken. He is speaking now.

———◆———

*I rise before dawn and cry for help; I have put my hope in your word. My eyes stay open through the watches of the night, that I may meditate on your promises.*
*Psalm 119:147-148*

*Lord, You are always speaking. Open my ears to hear your voice. Let me look to You above anyone else or anything else for comfort, courage, and guidance.*

# 79

*I fear that I'm turning negative. I'm finding
fault with everyone and everything lately.
I'm more critical and irritable.*

*I have little to no patience for anyone or
anything. I manage to hold it together in
public, but my heart is churning inside.*

*I'm certainly not happy. Joy seems to
have departed with my spouse.*

*My vision is clouded by my terrible loss. I used
to be optimistic. Not anymore. I might smile,
but inside I'm all doom and gloom. I tell myself
this isn't helpful or right, but my mind runs
down those dark, hopeless trails anyway.*

*I don't think I like who I'm becoming.*

---

The loss of a spouse can indeed cloud our vision. This death can darken our lenses and skew our thinking.

Ultimately, the Lord is the only one who sees with total clarity. He knows all, understands all, and is working with all the broken pieces in our lives to build something extraordinary.

It's hard to see this when our lenses are stained and we feel like we're in a pit filled with pain and grief. Our emotions are powerful and can be overwhelming.

God is with us in our pit. He knows every thought and feeling. He reminds us that now is not forever. He is at work. His arms are around you. Even though you walk in a dark, unfamiliar valley, God your shepherd is leading you to green pastures on the other side.

The only way out of grief is through it. Healthy grieving is the way forward.

———◆———

*Lord, be gracious to us; we long for*
*you. Be our strength every morning,*
*our salvation in time of distress.*
*Isaiah 33:2*

*You know all things, Lord. You know me. I belong to*
*You. I am yours. You are with me in this. I trust that*
*You are guiding me, even when I cannot perceive You.*

# 80

*I miss my spouse. I want to see them
and be with them so badly.*

*I never understood how someone could even
contemplate taking their own life. Well,
now I can see how that's possible.*

*Pain. I want relief from the pain. I want a break
from the constant cloud of mental haze, sadness,
and longing. It's like a 50-pound backpack that
I wake up with and carry around all day. I can
see why some would wonder if life is worth it.*

*I can imagine some seeing suicide as a way out. I guess
we all have our limits as to what we're willing to endure.*

*Someone told me I stare and sigh a lot. I'm
not surprised. I have a lot to sigh about.*

———◆———

Self-harming thoughts and behaviors are on the rise in our world. Suicide is becoming more acceptable. It's tragic that a forever decision that takes lives is becoming almost a trend, a fad, a meme.

Life is a gift. All living beings owe their existence to God. He is life and the author of all life. He even came, clothed Himself in human flesh, and died our death on the cross to ensure that life would win.

Our hearts want peace. I'm reminded again of what Jesus said, "I have said these things to you so that in me you may have peace." No one and nothing else can give us peace. When we attempt to replace Him with anyone or anything, our lives shrink and our hearts grow dark.

The loss of a spouse is traumatic. Peace amid the pain and confusion is found in Him. He is peace. Keep being real and honest with Him. His love for you is limitless.

———✦———

*For He Himself is our peace...*
*Ephesians 2:14*

*You are my peace. Move me to rest in You.*
*Let me experience your peace, Lord, more*
*and more with each passing day.*

If you're having suicidal thoughts, now or in the future, please involve someone you trust immediately. Call the suicide hotline at 1-800-273-8255, or text "home" to 741741.

# 81

*Well, I went to the support group.*
*I was pleasantly surprised.*

*Granted, I was terrified beforehand. I found*
*a dozen excuses not to go. But I got in the*
*car, drove there, breathed deeply, and walked*
*in trying to look halfway composed.*

*They were friendly. Everything was low*
*pressure. Some shared a lot. Some hardly*
*spoke. All of us teared up. Some cried.*

*I felt better afterwards. I didn't say much, but my heart*
*felt lighter. Perhaps some of my grief pressure got released.*

*I know these groups aren't a positive experience for*
*everyone. I'm glad my first attempt wasn't a disaster.*

---

Every support group is different. Each individual is unique. Though our grief is one-of-a-kind, being with others who are hurting from a loss can be comforting and reassuring. Relating to other widowed spouses can be especially helpful.

Fellow grieving hearts remind us that what we're experiencing is common. It's relieving to know we're not crazy. It's okay to not feel okay. Though our loss and grief are unique, connecting with other grievers sends our hearts the message that we're not alone in this.

Having said that, not all support groups are for everyone. Sometimes you have to try a few to find one that syncs with who and where you are.

God provides who and what we need. Some people might disappear on us, but others will rise to take their place.

He is our shepherd. He blesses us with the people we need.

———⋘⋙———

*Carry each other's burdens, and in this*
*way you will fulfill the law of Christ.*
*Galatians 6:2*

*Lead me, Lord, to supportive people. Let me be*
*safe and supportive for others. Connect me with*
*others who can walk with me in this grief.*

# 82

*I somehow feel a little better. I know that's not
a good measuring stick and that my emotions
can change with the next breeze, but it's nice to
have some relief from the constant cloud.*

*I'm writing a little more lately. I think that might
be helping too. My mind moves so fast that I thought
getting things down on paper might be good. It slows
my poor, spinning brain and forces me to focus.*

*As I write what's going on inside me, I try to
release it. I know it may boomerang back. That's
okay. I'll write it down and release it again.*

*I feel like I'm learning how to grieve. I
don't like it, but at least I'm not totally
hijacked by my emotions all the time.*

*Sigh. I miss my spouse. I love them so much.*

---

Writing can be incredibly cathartic. Whether it's an occasional expression of the heart, consistent journaling, or writing poetry or letters about or to our spouses, writing can be a wonderful way to process our grief.

You're right about our minds. They spin. Our thoughts ping here and there and then circle back again and again. Writing helps us focus and express what's happening inside us. Just getting it out is relieving and beneficial.

David did this frequently in the Psalms. In an intentional and concentrated way, he poured out what he was thinking and feeling. He processed his fear, doubt, emotional pain, and grief.

Writing is one more way we can be honest with ourselves and God.

———◆———

*I wait for the Lord, my whole being waits, and in His word I put my hope. I wait for the Lord more than watchmen wait for the morning...*
*Psalm 130:5-6*

*Move me to be honest with You, Lord. Let me hold nothing back. Bring healing to my soul as I walk this path of grief.*

# 83

*What you said about David expressing his heart
and grief to God in the Psalms was helpful. I
knew that, but it hadn't clicked before.*

*I decided to tweak how I write. Now, before I
begin writing and expressing what I'm feeling and
thinking, I write, "To God." In other words, I begin
by acknowledging that I'm sharing with Him.*

*So far, it's been great. I feel more connected. I'm
sensing His presence more. When I finish writing
an entry, I feel like God and I are in this together.
I know we are, but I haven't felt that way much.*

*My heart is still broken. I miss my spouse desperately.
I'm expressing to God my longings and my loneliness.
Knowing He is with me in this is a huge comfort.*

⸻

It sounds like your writing has become prayer. You're right.
God was already with you in this. He knew every thought and
emotion, but intentionally including Him and directing it to
Him sends a message to your own heart. The message is that
God is not only with you, but also that He cares.

God is listening. As you honestly express what's happening
inside you to Him, your heart begins to sense His companion-

ship. As you continue this, you will also experience more of His love and peace.

Yes, there will be ups and downs to this. There may be times when He seems a million miles away. Stay the course. Make Him your target and keep expressing your heart. Overall, this will lead to a closer sense of connection with Him.

"To God," is a wonderful way to start anything—writing, drawing, relating, eating, exercising, working, and living.

---

*And whatever you do, whether in word or deed, do it all in the name of the Lord Jesus, giving thanks to God the Father through Him.*
*Colossians 3:17*

*Lord, You are my life. You live in me. I live in You. Make my life about companionship with You. Lead me, my shepherd.*

# 84

*So much death. So much tragedy. I know it was there*
*before, but now I seem to be aware of it more.*

*Loss is everywhere. I see it on the news and*
*in the media. I'm hearing more about it*
*from neighbors, friends, and coworkers.*

*There is more to life than loss, isn't there?*

*I feel sad, a little stunned, and perhaps depressed.*
*I look at the world and don't see colors anymore—*
*only gray. My loss, the death of my spouse, is*
*only one among millions of other losses.*

*I don't want to be morose. I don't want to be thinking*
*about death. I want to grieve, but still engage in life.*
*I want to live well, but right now I'm not sure how.*

*It would be nice to feel joy again.*

When I was a college student, one of my mentors said, "Life is a series of losses." I nodded. I already knew this to be true. Then he continued. "How we interpret and respond to those losses makes all the difference." In other words, how we grieve and live after a loss matters deeply.

I have certainly found this to be accurate in my own experience. We live in a broken world full of wounded people. We experience loss after loss. If we don't find ways to trust God, grieve in healthy ways, and use these losses for good, the hits of life will end up defining us. We can't afford to let that happen.

You've lost your spouse – a huge, massive loss. You're in a season of grief. While in this season, you'll be especially sensitive to the loss and pain you sense around you. This is natural and common.

Breathe deeply and keep expressing your heart openly to the Lord. Process everything with Him.

In time, the color will return.

---

*Because of the Lord's great love, we are not consumed, for His compassions never fail.*
*Lamentations 3:22*

*Open my eyes and let me see things more from your perspective, Lord. I give You my pain and grief. Lead me through this valley. Comfort my heart.*

# 85

*The next support group meeting is today.*

*I'm feeling nervous already. I hadn't anticipated this. My first meeting was good, and I thought I would be looking forward to the next one. Instead, I find myself wanting to hide.*

*I'm not going to hide, however. I know now that almost everything healthy in this exhausting process of losing a spouse requires courage. Every step forward seems to be scary.*

*I will breathe deeply and go. I'm resolved to do what's loving for myself and those around me.*

*The facilitator recommended coming at least three times because each meeting is somewhat different, and some are better than others. That makes sense.*

*I may struggle throughout the day. That's okay. I'm going. I've made that decision. I will trust God with getting me there and with how it goes tonight. I'm not in charge. I never have been.*

*Breathe. Trust. Move.*

The struggle you're describing is common. Most grieving spouses get nervous when heading to support groups—or perhaps gatherings of any kind.

Widowed spouses can often feel their hearts shaking with grief—grief that needs to be expressed. It's trying to find its way out, and it begins to exert more pressure. This is natural.

You're right. Every step forward in healthy grieving takes courage. Another way to think of it is that healthy grieving requires us to exercise faith. We're not in control. We're completely dependent on God for life itself and all else. That can be scary. Being healthy demands that we embrace reality—as God enables us.

He is good. He is perfect. Trusting Him is the way to healing, recovery, and peace. He Himself is our peace and joy.

Growth and healing happen as we trust Him, one day, one moment, one step at a time.

---

*The Lord is my strength and my shield; my heart trusts in Him, and He helps me. My heart leaps for joy, and with my song I praise Him.*
*Psalm 28:7*

*God, help me to trust You. You are good. Your love endures forever. You are my life, my peace, and my joy. I cling to You.*

# 86

*The support group was good. I'm glad I went.*

*It was hard at times. I emoted more this time than last. The relieving thing was that I didn't feel embarrassed. Instead, I felt safe and free. Free to grieve.*

*I haven't felt that until now. It felt good. It felt right.*

*I wish there was another meeting tonight. I would be there. I'm learning. I need other people who "get it." I need people in my life who have lost spouses and know this grief. Safe people. Trustworthy and compassionate people.*

*Now that I've tasted some of the goodness of having my heart and grief respected, I want more. Much more.*

---

I believe God brings the people we need when we need them. For us, it's never soon enough, but He has His timing for all things.

So much of life—and grief—has to do with timing. We don't know when our hearts are ready for something, but God does.

He has a plan for you, and it's a good plan. He is working in all things to express His love and care for you. He has brought you into a circle of other caring, grieving hearts. And they have embraced you.

As we share our hearts authentically with others and are met with love and acceptance, we tend to feel loved and accepted by God as well.

We're designed to reflect God's loving, comforting, and encouraging nature, but the world entices us away from this. We get caught in demanding routines. We find ourselves surrounded by messages that cause us to construct our own little fortresses. We build walls to protect ourselves.

When we experience love and compassion from others, our walls tend to come down a little. We experience God's goodness through other people, and we want more. Much more.

---

*By this everyone will know that you are
my disciples, if you love one another."*
**John 13:35**

*Lord, bring safe and loving people into my life. Make me
a safe and loving person. Construct healing relationships
all around me. Thank you for your goodness to me.*

# 87

*I find myself wanting to give. After being in the support
group and hearing others' stories – especially from
other widowed spouses - my compassion is aroused.
I'm not alone. I'm not crazy either. I'm grieving.*

*And I have reason to grieve. But I don't have to stop
living. I'm starting to understand that grieving is living.*

*My job right now, above all my other responsibilities,
is to take care of myself by grieving in the
healthiest way possible. I feel selfish saying that.
It sounds so self-focused. Yet, as I care for myself
better, I can feel my heart responding.*

*I want to reach out more.*

———◆———

Being with others who know deep grief can have a profound
impact on us. God designed us for relationship. He often uses
other people to express His care and concern for us. It sounds
like He is doing that for you through this support group.

I rejoice with you. You're not alone and you're far from crazy.
You're missing someone incredibly special – your spouse. You're
grieving. And right now, grieving well and experiencing God
in the process is your heart's priority.

We can't give away what we don't have. As we care for and love ourselves well, it expands our capacity to love and serve others. Good self-care is honoring to God. He created you unique— one-of-a-kind in human history. You embrace this truth when you care for yourself well.

As you begin to treat yourself as God does—with compassion, kindness, mercy, forgiveness, and love—your heart will heal and your desire to give and serve will grow.

---

*"'Love the Lord your God with all your heart and with all your soul and with all your strength and with all your mind'; and, 'Love your neighbor as yourself.'"*
**Luke 10:27**

*Lord, You are love. You live in me. Let me experience your love more and more. Love others through me.*

# 88

*I've tended to put myself last. Everyone
and sometimes everything else came first.
Spouse. Kids. Work. Home. Then me.*

*I thought this was godly. I thought this was
what I was supposed to do—sacrifice myself
on the altar of everyone else. The result has
been fatigue, frustration, and now anger.*

*The terrible loss of my spouse and the resulting grief have
taught me I don't want to live that way anymore. How
can I give and serve if I'm not taking care of myself first?
How can I live from my heart when my tank is near
empty, and I'm running on fumes almost all the time?*

*Yet, I feel guilty. Perhaps I need
some sort of spiritual detox.*

---

A spiritual detox might indeed be a good idea.

We're taught to serve others and to pursue a lifestyle of love. This kind of life, however, requires that we live in faith and from our hearts. Solomon said, "Above all else, guard your heart, for it is the spring from which everything else in life flows." The heart is our most prized possession. If we lose it, we lose everything.

When we trusted God, He gave us a new heart. A heart of love, service, and impact. However, we are not superhuman. We exercise this heart God has given us by seeking Him and getting to know Him. Knowing Him better becomes our priority.

The better you know Him, the more you will heal and grow—and the more He will live through you. It's not about you doing it. It's about Him living in and through you to do what He wants to do when He wants to do it.

Most of us need a spiritual detox from time to time. As you reorient your life around knowing God, everything else tends to fall into place over time.

---

*I will give you a new heart and*
*put a new spirit in you...*
*Ezekiel 36:26*

*God, I want to know You better. Move me to focus*
*on You. Let my relationship with You flow into*
*all my other relationships. Heal me, Lord.*

# 89

*I've been thinking about the spiritual detox concept.*
*I think I've bought into some lies along the way*
*in my spiritual life. Those lies have driven me*
*along, exhausted me, and left me floundering.*

*Losing my love, my spouse, has brought some clarity.*
*I find myself questioning what I do and why. Why*
*do I do this or that? What's the motive behind how*
*I'm living? Over time, I've lost focus. My passion*
*has waned. This deep grief has sucked me dry.*

*Now that I'm dry, I can see the emptiness of how*
*I was living. I was going through the motions.*
*Scattered. Distracted. Chasing my tail.*

*I was on a never-ending treadmill. I*
*was moving but going nowhere.*

*The death of my spouse threw everything into confusion.*
*My personal electricity shut down and threw me*
*off the treadmill. It hurt terribly, but I'm realizing*
*I don't want to climb on that treadmill again.*

---

Our world is demanding. Responsibilities—both legitimate ones and those that we allow others and the world to place upon us—grow and multiply like weeds in a manicured lawn. Over time, activity and busyness hijack our lives.

God's voice speaks from the Psalms, "Be still and know that I am God." We don't like being still. We live in an age of instant everything. Constant information overload drives us. Noise fills our lives. We hurry everywhere. We're breathless. Our to-do list is never done.

Though hard and painful, this season of deep spousal grief can be a blessed time. God is calling. He wants to heal your heart, day by day, moment by moment.

———◆———

*"Be still and know that I am God; I will be exalted among the nations. I will be exalted in the earth."*
**Psalm 46:10**

*Lord, You are my life. I need a spiritual detox. I look to You. You are always speaking. Cause me to listen. I want to live from the new heart You have given me.*

# 90

*Somehow, I thought that life was about
activity. Doing things. Producing. Achieving.
Being responsible. Doing the right thing.*

*Yet, when I read the Bible, I sense something different.
Life isn't about me doing things, but about God
living in me and through me. It's not about me
trying to please Him, but about me trusting Him.*

*I feel like I need to stop and analyze everything
I thought was true. It's like I knew who God
was but didn't know Him very well.*

*I knew He loved me, but honestly, I was mostly
afraid of Him. Fear of doing something wrong kept
driving me to do what I felt was right. My heart
was out of sync. I was living from my head more
than from my heart. I kept God at a distance.*

*I'm sighing a lot again. I miss my spouse, and I don't
know what to do. Yet, I sense I'm on the right track.*

---

Grief tends to chip away at what we think we believe. What
we truly believe comes out in the way we live. The death of a
beloved spouse naturally brings a lot of things into question.
Our hearts tremble. Our souls can be shaken.

This can be a good shaking. If we're willing, this deep grief can lead us back to the Source—God Himself. Though we're in a mental fog, some things become clearer.

We're not the same people we were. We don't want to live like we did. Death has brought perspective. It can fuel in us a desire to live from our hearts in constant companionship with God. This is what we were designed for, but it often takes a tragedy or loss to get our attention.

This life and this world are not all there is. Thank goodness. We can live with eternity in mind. We can live from our hearts.

God is with you. You are part of His story. He is your life.

———◆———

*Jesus answered, "I am the way and the truth and the life. No one comes to the Father except through me."*
*John 14:6*

*God, I want to know You better. I want You to be the driving force behind my life and everything I do. Heal me and live through me, Lord.*

# 91

*I have discovered a big lie I was living. I thought I
was what I did. My accomplishments. Achievements.
My family and what I did for them.*

*I was caught in all my roles. Spouse, parent, co-
worker, employee, church member, friend, etc. I was
running and moving fast. What was I afraid of?*

*Deep down, maybe I was afraid of everything.*

*Now, I'm listening to my heart. Life is about God.
Everything else changes and eventually disappears.*

*I believe God gave me a new heart. I believe He lives
inside me. I sense He wants to live through me. Life
isn't about me or about anyone else. It's about Him.*

*I still don't know what to do with this. It's
like I'm waking up for the first time in a new
world. I miss my spouse desperately, but I sense
God is healing me, a little bit at a time.*

———⚜———

You're right. You're not what you do. You are so much more.

You were thought of, wanted, and planned by God. Jesus
Christ came and gave His life for you. He conquered death so
that He could give His life to you and live His life in you.

The universe is about Him. He designed and created it—and you. Life is about Him. He is life. He is eternal life.

He invites us to change the focus of our thinking from earthly things to Him. It's only in companionship with Him that we begin to understand who we are, what life is about, and why we're here. He brings perspective to things like death, loss, and grief.

If you've trusted in Christ to give you His life and invited Him to live in you, He has become your life. He is the ultimate grief expert. He walks with you. He is in you. You are in Him.

Even amid all the pain for this terrible loss, His love for you never changes.

Rest. Be still. Know that He is God.

———❖———

*We know also that the Son of God has come and has given us understanding, so that we may know Him who is true. And we are in Him who is true by being in His Son Jesus Christ. He is the true God and eternal life.*
*1 John 5:20*

*Lord, knowing You is everything. I heal as I get to know You better. I heal as I walk with You and receive from You. I heal as You live in and through me.*

# 92

*I keep having headaches and stomach issues. It has definitely gotten worse since my spouse died. Some days it's just annoying, but sometimes it's almost debilitating.*

*I've been to the doctor. They did some blood work and tests. Nothing. I figured. I'm betting it's all grief and stress.*

*I'm trying to let go of things that burden me. I'm attempting to grieve in healthy ways, but perhaps I'm failing.*

*The physical stuff is bad today, and I'm discouraged. I felt like I was making progress and taking some leaps forward. Now, I'm not so sure.*

---

The intense grief after the loss of a spouse is a form of stress, and our bodies feel it. The emotional demands are heavy, and our systems get taxed by the constant pressure. It can wear us down after a while.

Our bodies try to keep the stress at bay, but sooner or later we feel our grief physically. Many feel it every day. Headaches, stomach distress, palpitations, exhaustion, aches and pains, and more frequent illnesses are all common.

For some of us, our bodies don't feel the impact until we're processing our grief better. Our brains sense our healthy responses and send the message to our bodies that it's now safe to break down a bit and feel this grief. In other words, more physical distress doesn't necessarily mean you aren't doing well or grieving in healthy ways.

The answer is still the same. Grieve in healthy ways. Care for yourself in this. Let God love you. Rest in Him.

Grief is an unpredictable, windy, rock-strewn road. Walk with God. Let Him lead. He is your shepherd.

———

*Listen to my prayer, O God, do not ignore my plea; hear me and answer me. My thoughts trouble me and I am distraught.*
*Psalm 55:1-2*

*I feel vulnerable, Lord. I'm easily discouraged. My body is feeling the pressure of life and loss. Enable me to trust You. I release all burdens to You.*

# 93

*Life without my spouse is heavy and lonely. I try
to keep my focus on God. I remind myself that
whatever I face today, He can handle it.*

*I thought I could handle almost anything. Maybe I
considered myself invincible, in charge, and in control.*

*The reality is stunningly different. I am fragile, but God
is with me. I am broken, but God is healing me. I am
grieving, but God is walking with me in my pain. I am
dependent on Him for all and everything. He is good.*

*Yes, I know there's a lot of suffering in this
world. If He is not good, and if He is not
love, then I'm in trouble. We all are.*

*Lord, have mercy on us.*

---

I think again of Jesus' words, "In this world, you will have
trouble." Life is heavy. Loss, demands, and fear come knocking
frequently.

We are indeed fragile. We are imperfect. We are flawed and
sorely limited. God is our strength. He is our Rock and our
Fortress. His love and power are limitless.

You're right that we can't handle loss or life by ourselves. We
weren't meant to. In God, we can do all things, as He gives us

His strength. He lives in and through us. In ourselves, we can't. In Him, we can.

He is your resource, your hope, and your life.

The loss of a spouse is painful and heartbreaking. The Lord knows this. He knows you. He knows your heart. He meets you where you are and walks this lonely road with you.

———————

*"I am the vine; you are the branches. If you remain in me and I in you, you will bear much fruit; apart from me you can do nothing."*
*John 15:5*

*I am fragile and limited, Lord. You are my strength, my hope, my life. I live in You. You live in me. I will trust You and rest in You today.*

# 94

*I can't seem to get on top of things. I'm always
spinning. I used to be a good juggler, but
now I have too many balls in the air.*

*My concentration isn't what it was. I tell myself,
"It's okay. I'm grieving. This is common and
expected." That helps, but I don't like it.*

*I find myself wondering if this new life without my
spouse is ever going to get any better. Will the grief always
be this deep and intense? Does the heart ever rebound?*

*I know I won't be the same and I don't want
to be—but I would like to feel better.*

*Maybe I should just let some balls drop from
time to time. I can't keep them all in the air.
Perhaps I'm expecting too much of myself.*

---

We're certainly not the same people after the loss of a spouse.
Our lives are a web of relationships. When one strand—especially a thick, foundational one—is severed, the whole web
shakes with the shock. It takes time for the heart to find a new
equilibrium.

Our world has changed. As we grieve in healthy ways, we heal and grow. Yet, many of us are surprised by the power and duration of grief. Wanting to feel better is natural.

Grieving is an individual path unique to you, your heart, and your relationship with your spouse. There are patterns to grief, but no two grief paths are exactly the same. Therefore, there is no timeline. The grieving process takes as long as it takes.

The grief will end when you stop missing your spouse. That means that, on some level, you'll be grieving the rest of your life. As you heal, however, the grief will change over time.

Walking this grief road is part of trusting God. Keep expressing your heart to Him. He Himself is your peace, your patience, and your endurance.

As you grieve in healthy ways, you will be healing and growing. As much as possible, breathe deeply and walk with God in the present moment.

---

*Lord, my strength and my fortress,*
*my refuge in time of distress...*
*Jeremiah 16:19*

*You, Lord, are my strength, my peace, and my life.*
*I present myself to You today. I am yours. I trust*
*that You are leading, guiding, and healing me.*

# 95

*As I read the Scriptures, I keep running across verses
that say that Christ is in me and that I am in Him.*

*I've read these before, but they're hitting home
with me now. He's not just with me, but in
me. I'm not just with Him, but in Him.*

*I don't know what this means, but I want to
accept it as true. It sounds safe and comforting.*

*I want to experience this connection with God more.
At times, there seems to be a wide gap between what I
feel and what Scripture says. I want to experience God
Himself. I know I do, but I want more. I need more.*

*I want more of Him and His peace and joy amid
all this trouble and grief. I desperately need His
companionship to quell this terrible loneliness.*

---

All of us have a faith-experience gap. There are many things
that we believe—or say we believe—that we don't experience
much in daily life. Simply put, we wonder if God is so good,
why are things the way they are? If His love for us is perfect,
why do we feel as we do?

We're restless. On some level we should be. There is a godly
restlessness that occurs for many of us. We long to see our Cre-

ator face-to-face and be with Him completely. We hunger for heaven. Our hopes and dreams usually reveal this longing.

This world is not our home. We are citizens of heaven. God Himself is our home. No wonder we yearn. It's a sort of holy discontent.

As we walk with Him, we learn to experience more of Him here—His goodness, love, and comfort. We're content in Him, yet we long for more. We're longing for more of Him.

One day, we will be fully satisfied. For now, we yearn.

---

*Dear friends, now we are children of God, and what we will be has not yet been made known. But we know that when Christ appears, we shall be like him, for we shall see him as he is.*
*1 John 3:2*

*When I see You, Lord, I will be whole and fully satisfied. Until then, I yearn. My heart looks for total and complete healing. I have that in You. One day I will experience it.*

# 96

*I still wonder why I'm here sometimes. I
know that's ridiculous, because I know
why I'm here. God put me here.*

*I didn't decide to whom or when I would be born.
I don't cause my own heart to beat or my brain
to function. I don't control hardly anything.*

*The world feels so big, and I feel so small. Tiny.
Powerful forces seem to be behind everything,
driving events, situations, and people here and
there. When I realize this, I'm stunned.*

*Most of the time, I refuse to even go there. I
keep my head down, focus on my own agenda,
and don't concern myself with such things. All
the big stuff seems instantly overwhelming.*

*Who am I in all this? I'm alone now. How
do I make sense of this new life?*

*I wonder.*

---

The loss of a beloved spouse causes us to think about a lot of things.

We see life and events differently. Our hearts have been tender-ized. We're more sensitive to pain and suffering. Even though we still go through the motions, living on autopilot isn't good enough anymore.

Deep down, we want to live. We want to matter. We want our lives to count. We're hungering for God again.

We're created by Him and for Him. He alone knows our true and complete purpose. He gives each of us a unique calling and mission.

Whatever the calling or mission, however, it comes down to loving Him and loving people. We're wired to love and be loved.

He is love. He invites us to experience Him.

———◆———

*Being confident of this, that He who began a good work in you will carry it on to completion until the day of Christ Jesus.*
*Philippians 1:6*

*Lord, You are always at work in me. You will complete what You have started. I return to the basics today. I will focus on loving You by loving people. Work in and through me today.*

# 97

*I think I settle a lot.*

*I start out optimistic. I dream. I hope. And then reality sets in and downgrades my expectations. I cease to hope for more and settle for what is.*

*I know accepting the current reality is important. I miss my love, my spouse. I want them back. I still can't grasp a world without them.*

*But I don't want to grieve all the time. I want to live—and grieve well along the way. I don't want to let loss determine my life. I don't want to settle into some off-white, dull, small existence. I don't want to walk through life afraid of the next tragedy. I want to live and live well.*

*Those around me deserve this from me. How can I love them if I'm stuck in grief?*

---

We all seem to start as dreamers. Then we get disappointed, hurt, and wounded. Life begins to kick the optimism and imagination out of us. We become jaded. Careful. Cautious. Realistic.

In order to protect ourselves and those we love, we tighten our hearts. We try to control people and circumstances. We live our days guarded and hesitant. If we experience enough loss, we go internal. We hide.

We look at God differently too. Instead of a loving Father, He becomes a distant disciplinarian. Instead of intimate and deeply personal, we see Him as aloof and distracted—too busy with the grand affairs of the universe to pay too much attention to us.

Faith and trust are inherently risky. Yet, if God is who He says He is, He is ultimate safety. Our challenge is to see Him for who He is, rather than letting our minds recreate Him in our image based on what's happened to us.

Only God Himself satisfies. Only He can give us true perspective. He is our strength, our healing, our hope, and our life.

---

*Whom have I in heaven but you? And earth has nothing I desire besides you. My flesh and my heart may fail, but God is the strength of my heart and my portion forever.*
**Psalm 73:25-26**

*Lord, You are life. You are my home. You are my strength. All my longings are ultimately about You. Only you can meet my needs. Be my priority and my foremost desire.*

# 98

*I know God is good. That's what my mind tells me.*

*My heart is wounded. I can't feel His goodness sometimes, though I see it all around me.*

*The loss of my spouse has been heartbreaking. The emotional pain packs such a punch. Why does the negative seem to have more impact than the positive?*

*I can see now why some consider self-medicating—or even suicide. Life can be heavy, and depressing.*

*I guess we all self-medicate, don't we? One way or another, we all do less-than-healthy things to help ourselves feel better—myself included.*

*I've wondered before if it's worth it. Yes, I've had suicidal thoughts in the past.*

*Hopelessness and despair can be powerful indeed.*

---

Each of us carries personal pain. For some, the burden is heavy and crippling. There are times when our losses pile up and threaten to crush us.

When a spouse dies, we experience multiple, heavy losses. Everything changes. Only one strand is severed, but our entire life web is affected and forever altered.

Pain gets our attention. We're designed for relationship, not separation. We were created to connect and to love. Loss goes against the natural grain of our hearts. We live in a broken, loss-ridden, and pain-filled world.

God wants to give us peace in Himself amid all the turmoil and upheaval. Keep being real with Him. As much as possible, hide nothing. He knows anyway. Unburden your heart.

Breathe deeply and see yourself resting in God.

———————

*Surely God is my salvation; I will trust and not be afraid. The Lord, the Lord Himself, is my strength and my defense; He has become my salvation."*
**Isaiah 12:2**

*I rest in You, Lord. Though I feel shaky and uncertain, You are my fortress and my strength. Cause me to share all with You. I release my fears and worries now, one by one.*

# 99

*I bounce around emotionally. I used to be stable.
Now, without my spouse, I don't know.*

*One moment I can be okay and the
next moment I'm a mess.*

*Sad. Relieved. Irritated. Delighted. Frustrated.
Peaceful. Confused. Numb. I can be all of these,
and much more, in the span of a couple of hours.*

*I feel like I'm on a marathon roller coaster.
Just hanging on is exhausting.*

*I feel settled about God and His love for me, and
then my grief gets triggered and I'm suddenly
wondering about everything again. Emotional
upheaval has become my new normal.*

*I don't like all this unpredictability. I like
stability, but the ground under me is constantly
shifting. I have trouble keeping my footing.*

*I'm alone now. I'm tired. Life has worn me out.*

---

The loss of a beloved spouse shakes the heart terribly. Our emotions are stirred. Our internal Pandora's box of feelings pops open and out comes what appears to be a random, hodgepodge mixture of up-and-down and back-and-forth.

We're more sensitive. We feel more vulnerable. Life as we knew it has tilted, cracked, or even disappeared.

This is confusing, disorienting, and even frightening. Nothing feels settled, perhaps not even God and what we think or believe about Him. We're unsure of life and ourselves, and this uncertainty often extends to God too.

Be real with Him. He knows every twitch of your heart, every thought that passes through your mind. He feels your loneliness and walks with you in it. God loves you. Because of Jesus Christ and your trust in Him, God's acceptance of you is complete and total.

Breathe deeply. This emotional hijacking will diminish over time and eventually pass. Hang on. Trust.

---

*Your sun will never set again, and your moon will wane no more; the Lord will be your everlasting light, and your days of sorrow will end.*
*Isaiah 60:20*

*Help me remember, O Lord, that now is not forever. Things have changed and will continue to change, but You are always the same. I look forward to the end of this season of sorrow.*

# 100

*The loss of my spouse and my own issues
are more than enough to deal with. I don't
need everyone else's stuff on top of that.*

*The world is depressing. Trouble
everywhere. People acting crazy.*

*I sense anger. I see anxiety in people's eyes. It's
all too much. Too heavy for my small heart.*

*Maybe I'm thinking about things too much, but
what's happening around me is hard to ignore.
Can't we pause and let me catch my breath? I
can't handle my own life, much less any extras.*

*My own obligations feel like Mount Everest. I'm learning
to live in a constant state of fatigue, but I don't like it.*

*I miss my spouse. I feel like I need them
here with me, now, more than ever.*

---

We get bombarded with a stunning amount of information
every day, and little of it is positive or uplifting. Problems
abound. Life is tough. People are hurting.

We're hurting too – badly.

When we're in pain, sometimes all we can see is pain. Our

hearts have been broken open and every wind that blows through stirs our emotions. Perhaps we feel the pain of others more acutely. We're learning empathy through suffering. This is a good thing but draining at first. Feeling and sharing in the pain and suffering of others is part of love.

You've lost your love, your spouse. The pain is deep. Your heart senses the pain of others around you. This can feel overwhelming.

You're designed to be a reflection of God and His love to those around you. He lives in you. He is up to the task. Even when fatigued and exhausted, God can work in and through you in wonderful ways.

Breathe deeply. Lean into Him. Pour out your heart to Him. Rest. Trust.

---

*Surely God is my help; the Lord is*
*the one who sustains me.*
***Psalm 54:4***

*No matter what happens to me or around me, your love*
*for me is unchanged. You sustain me. You are my life.*
*I present myself to You. Use me today as you wish.*

# 101

*I can't believe I'm about to say this. At times, I have trouble remembering what my spouse looked like. I'm also having trouble remembering what their voice sounded like. This terrifies me.*

*When this happens, I rush to my phone and then to my computer. I look at old pictures. I watch a few videos. How could I ever forget their face or their voice?*

*What's happening? Am I that out-of-sight, out-of-mind? I feel guilty all over again. I can't believe they're gone. How can someone just disappear? Did all that really happen? Is this a dream?*

*If this is a dream, it's a nightmare. I'm ready to wake up.*

———◆———

Our spouse has a place in our hearts. When they depart, they leave a hole. That hole is reserved for them. Nothing and no one else can fill it. We're designed by God for relationships. This is part of what it means to be human.

What you're describing is common for grieving spouses. You're human. Like most of us, you tend to remember best what and who you're around the most. You're not forgetting your spouse. The loss is simply sinking into a deeper place in your heart.

You'll never forget them. Love endures. On some level, you'll always grieve. You miss them, but the intensity of the missing will change over time. This is part of healing. You're not distancing yourself from your spouse. The Lord is healing your heart.

Breathe deeply. Your heart is still in pieces. Be patient with yourself. Lean into God. He carries you.

———

*Love always protects, always trusts, always hopes, always perseveres. Love never fails.*
*1 Corinthians 13:7-8*

*Lord, no matter what I feel, your love is perfect. Thank you for loving me. Thank you giving me the ability to love. I give this pain to You.*

# 102

*I feel emotionally handicapped. My spouse is gone. It feels like half my heart – or more – has disappeared.*

*I move in a fog. I'm tired and can't seem to get on top of life. My spouse is never far from my mind. I miss them terribly. The hurt surfaces all over again.*

*Perhaps the pain is there all the time, just waiting for an excuse to show itself. I feel like a whiner. I despise it when others complain, but here I am, spewing my stuff everywhere.*

*Is there a difference between whining and venting? Are complaining and processing the same thing sometimes?*

*This is going to sound bizarre—I try to rest in God, but I'm too tired. I have so much on my mind and heart that I can't rest inside. My mind is spinning. My heart is bouncing all over the place.*

*Help.*

---

Things have changed. Your world has been altered. Your heart is rattled and desperately trying to regain its balance. Your mind has been stunned and is frantically searching for resolution. A huge, thick strand has been severed. Your life web is shaking.

Whether we call it whining, complaining, venting, or processing, it feels good and right to express our hearts—especially with those we feel safest with. Especially with God, the ultimate safe person.

He welcomes you today. All of you. All of you with all the mess. He's in this with you—loving and guiding you in ways you are not aware of.

Yes, rest is hard when you're spinning in circles. Breathe deeply and know that God is with you, in you, even as you spin. This too will pass. Keep being real with Him.

---

*For great is His love toward us, and the faithfulness of the Lord endures forever. Praise the Lord.*
*Psalm 117:2*

*No matter what my circumstances, Lord, You are with me. Even better, You are in me, and I am in You. I accept these truths today, even if I don't feel them much at present.*

# 103

*I want to experience God more. I want to be*
*used by Him in the lives of others. Honestly,*
*however, what I want most right now is relief.*

*I want peace. I want some answers. I want*
*energy to do daily life. I want some space.*

*There is no space out there. My life doesn't allow*
*it. Family, work, church, neighbors, finances—the*
*list goes on and on. All of me, all my time,*
*all my energy accounted for and gobbled up*
*before my feet hit the floor in the morning.*

*My spouse is gone. I'm alone in all this.*
*The heaviness of it all can be stifling.*

*I was busy before, but I didn't feel*
*like this. I'm exhausted.*

---

After the loss of a spouse, the resulting grief process is exhausting. Over time, fatigue skews our thinking. If sleep deprivation is the most basic form of torture, then long-term fatigue can have some debilitating results.

The answer is not to flee fatigue. We naturally feel what happens to us and around us. When a beloved spouse dies, our hearts grieve deeply. That grief can take up huge amounts of space. Suddenly, life takes much more energy than before. Again, this is natural. Common. Normal.

Grief cannot be effectively avoided. It is meant to be felt and processed over time. Your heart is your most prized possession. It needs your patience and kindness right now. Most of us have to do less when we're grieving. You're human and no exception to this.

Your only task is to receive from God and walk with Him. He can handle your life. He can manage your responsibilities.

Breathe. Experience His presence and His love. He is your life, your soul's oxygen.

───•❖•───

*You, God, are my God, earnestly I seek you; I thirst for you, my whole being longs for you, in a dry and parched land where there is no water.*
**Psalm 63:1**

*Lord, I seek You. Order my routine. Help me make decisions that build space into my life and heart. Refresh me, Lord.*

# 104

*I'm not at my best right now. Far from it.*

*I believe in excellence. I'm used to giving it my all and doing things well. I'm not sure I'm doing anything well right now. My spouse, my other half, is gone. I feel like a shadow of my former self.*

*I never knew loss could feel like this. I guess I imagined grief would be more manageable, or perhaps more definable. I never expected this much upheaval and vulnerability.*

*I want to give God my best, but that's not much right now. I don't feel like I have anything to give.*

---

You don't have to be at your best to experience God's love and goodness. You don't have to be on the top of your game for God to work through you and use you. You just need to be willing.

The truth is that God can work in and through us when we feel weak, powerless, and sad. He can use a broken and exhausted heart to bring comfort and peace to others. He routinely shows Himself through our weaknesses and even what we think are failures.

He is teaching you. He is guiding you. He is expressing His

love for you, moment-by-moment. Yes, I know your feelings lag behind these realities. That's okay. Anchor yourself in God's facts, and your feelings will eventually catch up.

━━━◆◆◆━━━

*Therefore, since we have been justi-
fied through faith, we have peace with
God through our Lord Jesus Christ.*
*Romans 5:1*

*On my worst day, Lord, You still love me completely.
I have peace with You, even when I do not feel it.
You live in me. Live through me, as You wish.*

# 105

*Nothing feels right lately. I seem to be
out of sync. Something's wrong.*

*Maybe it's all me. Perhaps I'm wrong. The
loss of my love, my spouse, has really messed
with me. I don't know which end is up.*

*And then perspective will come again. My heart will
settle a little. I get some peace. But then daily life
chases it away. I'm glad to be busy, and yet I don't
have time or energy to process much of anything.*

*The more fatigued I am, the more my mood rules
me. Feelings hijack me and begin to drive my life.
My emotions can be so strong and powerful.*

<hr>

You're right. Emotions are powerful. In our world, we often get things backwards. Feelings rule. Mood is king. If it feels right, we think it's true. If it feels good, we believe it. Feelings can end up driving our faith.

God's growth process for us is the other way around. It begins with facts—things He has revealed about Himself, us, and life. We accept and believe these things, though at times our feelings might not totally line up with God's facts. As we let facts drive our faith, our feelings eventually begin to follow.

We are emotional beings. God created us this way. Our feelings are meant to be felt, but not necessarily bowed down to.

Be aware of your feelings. Acknowledge the emotions. Breathe deeply. Process what needs to be processed. As you do, the feelings will begin to take their proper place in the scheme of things.

---

*I have been crucified with Christ and I no longer live, but Christ lives in me. The life I now live in the body, I live by faith in the Son of God, who loved me and gave Himself for me.*
*Galatians 2:20*

*My life is not about me. Lord, I give You my feelings. Focus me on You and your truth. I want to live by faith. Immerse me in your facts.*

# 106

*I've been thinking about the power of emotions.
I do tend to give them too much credit and way
too much influence in my life. They're important,
but not my guide and driving force in life.*

*Feelings can be beautiful. I have great memories with
my spouse. I smile at them. Those same memories
also bring tears. I'm deeply aware of what I've lost.*

*I'm thankful for those memories, though right
now they might bring pain. I think the pain is
already inside me and the memories are gifts from
God to help me release the pain and heal.*

*Why do life and loss have to be so emotional?
My feelings are such a jumble that sometimes
I have difficulty knowing what I'm feeling at
any given time. It can be so confusing.*

---

In grief and in life, we tend to let emotion drive our lives. We put feelings first and allow them to greatly influence or even determine what we do and what we believe.

Part of life's battle is to turn this around and let God's facts lead the way. As we know Him better, our faith forms, and eventually our feelings follow.

Choosing to believe God and His facts, even when we're conflicted emotionally, grounds us—in a good way. He becomes our anchor. We're no longer tossed here and there by every wind of emotion that blows through. Gratitude surfaces. Memories become priceless treasures.

As much as possible, let your mind dwell on what is good. Embrace the memories. Feel the emotions. Process the thoughts. Feel your steady anchor. Breathe deeply and know you are safe.

***

*Praise be to the God and Father of our Lord Jesus Christ, who has blessed us in the heavenly realms with every spiritual blessing in Christ.*
*Ephesians 1:3*

*No matter how I feel at any given moment, I have been blessed with every spiritual blessing in You, Lord. You are life. If I have You, I have everything.*

# 107

*I know I've said this before. One of the
disconcerting results of losing my spouse is that
it has introduced me to the stark reality that
anything can happen to anyone at any time. Even
to me. Even to others I love and care about.*

*I don't feel as safe anymore. I stay busy and
distracted, but in quieter moments the uncertainty
of life descends on me like a load of bricks.*

*I figure it's better to admit these thoughts and
get them out there. The alternative is to ignore
and bury them. I choose to expose them in the
hopes that they won't take root and produce fruit
that doesn't help me or those around me.*

*Am I safe now? How safe? What is safety, anyway?*

---

To heal and grow, we need a sense of safety. When we lose a spouse, our sense of security can be deeply shaken. We can begin living in fight or flight mode. Fear, rather than faith, can become the fuel that propels us.

I think again of Psalm 23. Even though we walk through the dark, unfamiliar, and frightening territory of spousal grief, we need not fear evil. Our shepherd is with us. He guides and protects. He heals and leads. He carries us. He surrounds us.

We live in an imperfect and broken world where pain and loss appear to rule at times. Death can give us perspective. This life is not all there is. It is but the introduction to eternity.

We are forever beings, created by God for God. He feels our pain. He comforts us. He has experienced death. He died for us, in our place. He gave His life for us so that He might live His life in us. Life is about Him.

He is life. He is ultimate safety.

---

*On my bed I remember you; I think of you through the watches of the night. Because you are my help, I sing in the shadow of your wings. I cling to you; your right hand upholds me.*
*Psalm 63:6-8*

*Lord, when I don't feel safe, move my heart to seek You. Let me know You are with me. Let me experience your love and safety.*

# 108

*If God is ultimate safety, and I know Him,
how come I don't feel safe? Is it because I
feel so lonely without my spouse?*

*Wait. I'm back to feelings again, aren't I? If God tells
me I'm safe, then I'm safe, no matter what I might feel.
My feelings are valid, but they aren't always reality.*

*I trust that God is true and right. He has me. I am
safe. The more I believe I'm safe and trust what
God has said, the more I will begin to feel it.*

*Facts, faith, and then feelings. I think I'm getting it.*

*In the heat of the battle, all this flies out the window, of
course. I'll let that be okay, and trust that God is training
me over time. Growth and healing take time, don't they?*

*I'm so impatient sometimes.*

———◆◆◆———

Living life well begins with knowing the truth. God Himself is
ultimate truth. All truth flows from Him. He is life. When we
embrace Him as our life, things begin to make more sense.

The Bible is full of verses about our safety. God is faithful.
He is committed. He is love. He doesn't forsake or abandon.
Unthinkable tragedies may happen, but we are eternally and
spiritually safe in Him.

Picture yourself in Him. Scripture says if you've trusted in Christ, He lives in you and you in Him. All things have been created by Him and for Him and through Him and in Him all things hold together. He is perfect. His safety is perfect.

In this world, we will have trouble—lots of it. He has overcome the world. You live in Him. He lives in you. You are loved. You are safe.

---

*The Lord will guide you always; He will satisfy your needs in a sun-scorched land and will strengthen your frame. You will be like a well-watered garden, like a spring whose waters never fail.*
*Isaiah 58:11*

*No matter how things might seem, You love me perfectly. I am safe and secure in You. You are safety and security. Help me to trust You.*

# 109

*Life is a struggle. The routine is merciless and demanding. Nothing slows down to allow for pain and loss – even the loss of a soulmate and life partner.*

*Everyone is busy about their business, unaware of the grief around them. Perhaps most people are unaware of their own grief. Maybe they don't want to face it.*

*I can understand that. Ignoring it sounds good, but that is not the path of healing. I would be hiding from myself and God.*

*I see sadness in the eyes of others now. I believe my support group has a lot to do with this. Being with others who are openly grieving gives my heart room to feel, emote, and vent. The release is good, and probably more important than I realize.*

*As I verbalize and process my own loss and grief, there seems to be more space in my heart to see others.*

*I still miss my spouse desperately. Maybe I always will. But the pain is different. It's a shared pain somehow. I've let others in. And I'm willing for others to let me in.*

---

We're designed by God for relationship. We're wired for connection with Him and with other people. Loss and separation are hard and painful – especially the death of a spouse.

When we're able to authentically share our pain and be heard, we feel loved. When we experience love, we heal a little bit.

God is love. Even if all others avert their faces and avoid us, we're still the ongoing recipients of perfect, limitless love. We can't feel the full delight of this, but we can taste minuscule bits of it, and those little bits of perfect love add up over time.

Some of us are more isolated than others. I believe, however, that God places safe, loving people around us. We just need eyes to see them and hearts receptive enough to engage. Many attempt to ignore and stuff their grief, but it will always be expressed, one way or another. It doesn't go away. Grief is meant to be felt.

You've said it well. Our pain is a shared pain. There is One who feels what we feel. He knows. He understands. Even if there are times we can't feel it, He is still the Father of compassion and the God of all comfort.

*"But now, Lord, what do I look for? My hope is in you."*
*Psalm 39:7*

*Many are hurting, Lord. You are hope and healing. Move hearts to seek You. Make me more aware of You. Let me see You everywhere.*

# 110

*When I talk to other widowed spouses, we all seem
to be experiencing frustration in our relationships.*

*I know I've talked about this before. People we
counted on disappeared. People avoid us. People act
like we've got some infectious disease. People don't
seem to know what to do with us, even though they
too have experienced loss in life of some kind.*

*I don't get it. Can't people just be kind and
compassionate? What's so hard about that?*

*I now know quite a few people who feel rejected and
abandoned by friends, co-workers, and even family.
People they thought cared about them and who promised
support. Frustrating. This adds insult to injury.*

*The death of our spouses was more than enough.
None of us needed more loss on top of that.*

---

People react to grief in strange ways. You're right. Every person
has experienced loss and pain. And yet our willingness and
ability to connect with and love others when they're hurting
seems severely limited.

Perhaps there's a basic human principle operating here. We
avoid pain. Our own pain. Others' pain. The world's pain.

We've had enough and seen enough. We don't want any more, so we pretend it's not there.

We're all imperfect, fallible, and prone to selfishness. Our heart space is limited, and if we haven't grieved prior losses in healthy ways, we will not respond well to loss in the lives of those around us. We'll make light of it, try to fix it, or run.

Developing the skill of forgiveness is more important than any of us can truly appreciate. God knows all about being ignored, rejected, and betrayed. He experiences these things continually. We're in good company.

---

*Finally, brothers and sisters, rejoice! Strive for full restoration, encourage one another, be of one mind, live in peace. And the God of love and peace will be with you.*
*2 Corinthians 13:11*

*You, Lord, are the forgiveness expert. You live in me. Enable me to forgive quickly. Love those around me through me, even while my heart is shaking.*

# 111

*I want to talk more about people and relationships.*
*I find myself getting angry, not just for myself,*
*but for others and how they're being treated by the*
*world and those immediately around them.*

*People can be cold. Mean. Even unfeeling. I don't*
*understand. How can they be like that? And many of*
*them call themselves Christians. How can this be?*

*Going to church has been hard at times. It stirs*
*my heart to the depths, and I'm very aware*
*of who's missing. The empty space next to me*
*is a constant reminder of my spouse.*

*Some people are supportive, but some aren't. Most*
*don't seem to know what to do with me.*

*Other grieving spouses I talk to express the same things.*
*People just stare. They blabber something belittling*
*and then walk away. Or they avoid us altogether.*

*No wonder I feel so alone.*

---

One of our general expectations in life is that we should be treated with kindness and respect. If not this, at least some common human decency would be appreciated.

Someone has said that an expectation is a disappointment

waiting to happen. After the death of a spouse, we're more vulnerable and certainly expect the usual engagement and kindness. When that doesn't happen, we feel robbed, cheated, and even abused.

At some point, we come to the place where we decide whether our expectations of others are realistic. And even if they are realistic, are we setting ourselves up for disappointment by having these expectations in the first place?

Releasing those around us from our usual expectations helps guard our hearts at this tender time. This can also turn our attention away from people's reactions and toward God's love and understanding.

Releasing our expectations of those around us can also motivate us to pursue safe people who know grief well.

Look to the Lord. He is your life, your hope, and your safety. He is your constant companion.

---

*But we have this treasure in jars of clay to show that this all-surpassing power is from God and not from us. We are hard pressed on every side, but not crushed; perplexed, but not in despair…*
*2 Corinthians 4:7-8*

*There are times, Lord, when some relationships seem impossible. I will guard my heart and trust You. Help me to release those around me of any unrealistic expectations I might have.*

# 112

*I've been moaning about the lack of compassion
in the world. I've judged those around me for
their lack of understanding. And then a friend
reminded me that I wasn't the most compassionate
soul on the planet when they lost their spouse.*

*I was stunned. I thought I was being supportive. I didn't
realize how I was coming across. Turns out that I was
guilty of most of what I've been judging others for.*

*This was humbling, but good. At first, I was mad.
Then I accepted the truth. I'm not perfect. Far
from it. I have been guilty at some time or other
of most of what I complain about in others.*

*I'm sorry, Lord. I confess this to you. I feel guilty.*

———◆———

What you've said is true for most of us. We're guilty—either
now or in the past—of most of what irritates us in others.

Ever since the Garden of Eden, we've been complaining about
the behavior of others and trying to fix their issues rather than
looking at our own hearts and dealing with ours. We have no
right or place to judge, and yet we do.

When confronted with our lack of love and compassion, we
typically either laugh it off and keep judging others, or we al-

low the truth to humble us. God's goal is not to mire us in guilt, but rather free us of unhealthy thoughts and actions.

He is love. He is eager to love us by loving others through us. When we judge, we block this process.

God's forgiveness is complete. Jesus' sacrifice for us is perfect. Instead of wallowing in guilt, we confess. We receive God's forgiveness. We get up and allow Him to love through us. This brings healing, both to others and our own hearts.

———◆———

*Blessed are the merciful, for they will be shown mercy. Blessed are the pure in heart, for they will see God. Blessed are the peacemakers, for they will be called children of God.*
*Matthew 5:7-9*

*Lord, you are merciful. You live in me. Extend your love and mercy through me to all around me. I want to be pure in heart – a peacemaker.*

# 113

*After yesterday's gentle confrontation, I
remembered more about how I responded
to people in the past in times of loss.*

*I've thought most of the unhelpful things that
others have said to me. I probably even said some
of them. I didn't understand, and I was running
from their pain rather than meeting them in it.*

*I'm trying to release the guilt when it comes, focus
on God's forgiveness, and learn from this. I'm
determined now to be different. I'll be compassionate.
I'll be part of God's comfort for hurting people.*

*I'll try to be more merciful toward those who
disappear, critique, judge, and say unhelpful
things. I'll pray for them. They have pain too.*

*The loss of my spouse is teaching me many things.*

We're all guilty of most of what we dislike in others. Perhaps
we see ourselves and are expressing our frustration that we are
the way we are.

We all run from pain. After all, who would run toward it? And
yet, Jesus, knowing what was ahead of Him, resolutely fulfilled
His mission and laid down His life for us.

He lives in us. He wants to live through us and express His sacrificial love. We are His ambassadors and emissaries of His comfort and healing.

We can enter others' lives and meet them where they are— in all the mess. This is an honor and a privilege. We can give away what we have received—love, forgiveness, patience, kindness, comfort.

Such compassion comes from the Lord Himself. Walk with Him in the present moment. He is your help and healing.

*We are therefore Christ's ambassadors, as though God were making His appeal through us.*
*2 Corinthians 5:20*

*I receive your forgiveness, Lord, for the unkind things I have thought and said when others were in pain. I am your ambassador. Live through me in compassion to others.*

# 114

*I want to make a difference. I want to use all this pain and grief for good.*

*I keep thinking I need to be doing better to be of any help to others. Have I healed enough to be of any benefit? I don't know.*

*When is enough healing enough? What does "doing better" look like now? When have I progressed enough that I can be used by God to bring solace and comfort to others?*

*I try, but sometimes my own grief gets in the way. Their pain triggers mine. I can make things about myself again in a heartbeat.*

*I miss my spouse desperately. I want this grief and loneliness to count somehow.*

———◆———

Thankfully, we don't have to be doing well for God to use us. He delights in expressing His love to and through us when we're at our worst and weakest.

Life is not something we can plan and expect to work out as we have envisioned. After losing your spouse, you know this all too well. We don't know what's going to happen or when.

Loving God, ourselves, and others is a dynamic, moment by moment, ever-changing process.

Our best bet is to simply stay focused on God as much as possible. We're constantly receiving all good things from Him. As we walk with Him, we naturally give away what we have received—love, goodness, comfort, compassion, etc.

As our grief gets triggered, we grieve together with those we're serving. It's not about getting it right. It's about giving and receiving love. It's about receiving what God has for us and letting Him live through us to those around us.

God is always at work. He is the Comforter. He lives in you. He will live through you today.

———

*For we are God's handiwork, created in Christ Jesus to do good works, which God prepared in advance for us to do.*
*Ephesians 2:10*

*You thought of me, wanted me, and created me. I am your handiwork. I will rest in You and trust that You work in and through me for your good pleasure.*

# 115

*This grief journey seems so long and challenging. Every day brings reminders. I miss my spouse terribly.*

*I'm thankful for my support group and for the people who are loving me amid all my personal chaos. They're not perfect, and they mess up from time to time. I do too. We're in it together. That's huge.*

*A safe person's presence is powerful. It's easier to believe God loves me when people do.*

*I'm finding ways to get around helpful people more and limit my exposure to unhelpful or toxic influences. I'm learning to guard my heart. That feels good.*

*I need inspiring, encouraging, and compassionate souls in my life. I'm healing, but I still need lots of understanding and acceptance. I guess I need that all the time, don't I?*

---

Love and acceptance are like oxygen to our souls, especially after the death of a spouse. We need a sense of safety to heal and grow. People who give us this gift are treasures indeed.

It's good to be aware of where we are. We're on the grief path. As we process our pain, we begin to heal. Healing takes time.

Our wounds can be deep. There are plenty of ups and downs and unforeseen obstacles on this path. We get surprised from time to time. We need patience from ourselves and from others.

God often reveals Himself through the presence and actions of safe, loving people. He teaches us to guard our hearts. He heals us, though we are never the same. We grow.

Keep letting God bring healing to your heart and mind. He is good. He loves you.

---

*Now that you have purified yourselves by obeying the truth so that you have sincere love for each other, love one another deeply, from the heart.*
*1 Peter 1:22*

*Lord, help me to be real with You, myself, and other people. Give me the reassurance I need. Plant your patience in me and cause it to grow.*

# 116

*I feel so lonely. I'm beginning to want companionship.*

*I feel guilty just saying that. I wonder if I'm being
unfaithful just because I want to talk, be heard,
listen, laugh, and connect with someone.*

*Wanting this is natural, right?*

*One moment, my heart says, "Go ahead. Try it."
The next thought is, "What are you thinking?"*

*I don't know how to feel. I don't know what to do.*

*Other people urge me to go ahead. They want me
to feel better and to move on. They have no idea
how emotionally complicated this is for me.*

*Complicated. Yes. Very.*

---

Wanting companionship is natural and healthy. God created us in His image as relational creatures. We seek to love and be loved. We thrive on interaction and acceptance. We need to be seen, heard, and known.

When our closest, most intimate companion departs, they leave a huge void. The heart needs time, usually quite a bit of time, to adjust to that massive empty space.

If you choose to seek companionship, you can help guard your heart by setting good boundaries. Setting clear expectations and communicating them well is key. This helps avoid complicating your grief process with more relationship stress.

If an invitation comes to you, please take your time. Resist the natural FOMO (Fear of Missing Out). God is sovereign. He knows your needs. Let Him lead.

Rest in Him. He is always with you - your ultimate companion.

———◆———

*Wait for the Lord; be strong and take heart and wait for the Lord.*
*Psalm 27:14*

*Lord, You are my ultimate companion. I set my heart on You. Guide me. I trust in You.*

# 117

*I've mentioned before how hard it is to go to church now. Don't get me wrong. I enjoy it. Well, parts of it. I want to be there. But it's not like it was.*

*My spouse isn't there, and everything seems to remind me of them.*

*My heart is different now. I'm different. Grief seems to hit me at church more than any other singular place.*

*Some ask me how I'm doing. Others avoid me. I feel like I'm wearing a sign, "Grieving spouse here. Approach at your own risk."*

*I need the connection, but I find myself wanting to get in and get out as quickly as possible. I want to be there, but I don't want to have to manage all these nutty emotions the entire time.*

*What do I do with all this?*

---

When we go to worship, we naturally go to open our hearts and connect with God and others. The music, prayers, and message are designed to speak to our hearts and souls.

Your heart has been deeply wounded. Your soul may feel a bit battered, even shaky. You've been hit hard by the loss of your life partner, and you're recovering. Your heart is cracked, and emotion naturally spills out everywhere.

Ideally, a gathering of other believers is a safe place. However, certain cultural expectations of what's appropriate and what's not come into play when we walk through the door. No matter what's happening inside, happy smiles proclaiming the message "I'm great!" are the usual fare.

Because you're hurting, you might feel out of sync. This is natural and common. Let it be what it is. Take care of your own heart as best you can.

Let church be, as much as possible, about the Lord. Breathe deeply and listen for His voice. He is with you, next to you, in you.

———◆———

*Because your love is better than life, my lips will glorify you. I will praise you as long as I live, and in your name I will lift up my hands.*
**Psalm 63:3-4**

*Set my heart on You, Lord. I am far too distracted by how I feel about what's happening around me. Set my mind on heavenly things.*

# 118

*I've concluded that it's okay if I'm
uncomfortable in church.*

*After all, how could I not be uncomfortable? My
spouse is gone. My life is completely different. I
feel lonely and out of sync with everyone else.*

*Uncomfortable doesn't mean bad. It
just means uncomfortable.*

*Looking back, it was in the uncomfortable times that
I matured and grew spiritually. That doesn't mean
I like it, but it certainly seems to be the truth.*

*I know there may be times in worship that are
particularly difficult. I'll be patient with myself
and loving toward myself during those moments. If
I need to step out or leave, so be it. That's okay.*

*The Lord knows my heart. He knows I love Him. He
knows I want to be with Him. He knows I need His
Word, His comfort, and the fellowship with others.*

*He knows. I want to trust Him.*

---

Yes, He knows. And you're right: we rarely grow when we're comfortable. Comfort zones feel good, but they don't bring comfort. Instead, they anesthetize our hearts.

When all is well and no trouble is visible on the horizon, we tend to settle into mediocrity and small living. God calls us to something greater: Faith.

You're trusting God as you walk in this deep valley of grief. He honors this. He delights in your worship, adoration, and trust. He is with you, in you, as you face feeling isolated and less than happy amid all the smiling Sunday faces. He walks the halls with you. He occupies your seat with you. He loves and accepts you as you are.

Yes, uncomfortable is okay. Focus on abiding in Him. Make Him your home no matter where you are or what you're doing. He is your life. He is your shepherd.

———— ❖ ————

*The Sovereign Lord is my strength; He makes my feet like the feet of a deer; He enables me to tread on the heights.*
*Habakkuk 3:19*

*Though life might be uncomfortable, I will trust that You are guiding and leading. You love me. I will rest in your love and receive from You.*

# 119

*If I can stop making things about
me, I do so much better.*

*For example, when I go out in public, instead of
concerning myself with how things are going to go
and how others will respond to me, I try to focus
on seeing others. I want to intentionally take an
interest in each person that engages with me. I
want to take the spotlight off myself and place
it where it should be—on those around me.*

*My spouse is gone, but I'm still here. I'm here to love. I'm
here to do good. I'm here to be a reflection of my Father
in heaven. I wish I could do this consistently. I feel like
an infant learning to move or stand up. I totter and fall
a lot. I go back to crawling because it's what I know.
Making everything about me is as natural as breathing.*

*It feels good when I get out of my own head
and notice what and who's around me.
I'm living again, at least a little.*

---

We live in a selfie world where we're encouraged to make everything about us. Imagine a city street full of people all taking selfies. They smile, laugh, and pose, but no one is aware of what's happening around them. No one is connecting. Everyone is self-focused, living in their own head.

Sadly, that's close to reality. As humans, we come out of the womb self-focused and then develop self-centeredness into our own personal art form. We make life all about us. God meant for life to be so much more.

I'm proud of you. Love begins with turning our hearts outward. It starts with setting our minds on the Lord and on engaging authentically with the world around us.

You are indeed a reflection of your Father. You were created in His image, and then recreated in Christ. You are a new creation now. Jesus lives in you, and He is love. As you trust Him, He lives and loves through you.

---

*Do nothing out of selfish ambition or vain conceit. Rather, in humility value others above yourselves, not looking to your own interests but each of you to the interests of the others.*
*Philippians 2:3-4*

*Live through me, Lord. Love those around me through me. Make each day count. Let my life be about You.*

# 120

*This morning, I found myself reading in 1 Corinthians
13 – a passage about love. I smiled and thought of
my spouse. As I read, the tears began to flow.*

*Love is patient and kind. It doesn't envy or boast. It's not
proud or self-centered. It doesn't run others down or hold
grudges. It sees evil for what it is. It rejoices in the truth.
Love protects, trusts, hopes, perseveres, and never fails.*

*I always thought this is how I should be. And
it is. But today I realized that these verses
describe God's love. This is how He loves me.
He is for me, always seeking my good.*

*I've been bogged down by grief and circumstances.
Life without my spouse has been exhausting
and heavy. Grief has worn me out.*

*And yet, I'm loved.*

*I'm loved with a perfect love by a perfect Father.
I miss my spouse terribly, but I can rest.*

———◆———

The loss of a spouse can lead us to appreciate love even more.
Our pain can remind us to look to Him who is love – God
Himself.

We were created to experience God and His perfect love and

then reflect Him and His love to others. When we know and begin to actually believe that we are loved by Him (and begin to live like we're perfectly loved by a perfect Father), our lives make some dramatic shifts.

We begin living outside ourselves and our own heads. We begin to flee from comparison and other dangers to our hearts. We immerse ourselves in what God has said about Himself, us, others, and life.

The better we know Him, the more we naturally reflect Him. The more we know and trust Him, the more He expresses Himself in and through us. Over time, we become more of who we were meant to be— who we really are. New creations. Children of the King. Heirs of an Eternal Father.

Receive His love. Bask in it. Release all worries and fears into His capable hands. Immerse yourself in Him.

---

*This is love: not that we loved God, but that he loved us and sent His Son as an atoning sacrifice for our sins.*
*1 John 4:10*

*I receive your love today. Fill me. Let your love build in me and then flow out of me onto all those around me. Love through me, Lord.*

# 121

*I woke up this morning thinking about God's love. I realized that I haven't felt it as much as I would like to.*

*When my spouse died, I think I somehow distanced myself from God. Apparently, I tie His love to my circumstances. If things are going well, it's easier for me to say that He loves me. If things are hard or painful, I wonder what's wrong and where He is in all this.*

*My circumstances change, but He does not. Do I see Him as responsible for all the painful stuff? I don't think so, but then I act like He's stopped blessing me and has turned His back on me somehow.*

*I'm sorry, Lord. I miss my spouse. Life seems completely different now, and I don't like it. My feelings about You seem to vary with each passing breeze.*

---

We tend to be emotion-driven creatures. If we like what's happening, we talk about God's love and goodness. In times of loss and confusion, we wonder where He went and why He allowed this to happen.

Breathe deeply. You're human. You're imperfect, fallible, and limited. You're enduring a massive loss – the loss of your beloved spouse.

God has you. The fact that you are thinking about these things is proof that He is working in your mind and heart.

The road of life is full of unpleasant, unexpected events and situations. God is still your shepherd. His love for you is unwavering. He is leading, protecting, and blessing you, moment by moment. There will be difficult places we must pass through, but there will be more green pastures ahead.

It's about trust. As we learn to trust Him in times of uncertainty, our hearts open up to experience His love in those times.

You're learning. He's training you in faith and trust. You're growing. He knows your heart. His love for you is perfect and unchanging. And there's nothing you can ever do to cause Him to love you any more or any less.

---

*For you created my inmost being; you knit me together in my mother's womb. I praise you because I am fearfully and wonderfully made; your works are wonderful, I know that full well.*
*Psalm 139:13-14*

*You thought of me and wanted me. You created me in my mother's womb. I belong to You. Your love for me is perfect. Reassure me of your love, Lord.*

# 122

*I'm still thinking about how closely I tie how I feel about what's happening to me and around me to God's love for me. I guess I see God's love as either fickle or conditional. I don't know. It's frustrating.*

*I know the issue is with me. I can either believe and trust that God's love for me is perfect, or I can focus on my circumstances and emotions. I can let His truth rule my heart or allow myself to be blown about by every new wind of mood and emotion.*

*I'm frustrated with myself. Am I that addicted to feeling good? Is my hunger for comfort and pleasant circumstances that strong?*

*At the same time, I do want to feel better. I feel lonely and sad. I'm tired of grief.*

*Then again, I feel guilty if I'm joyful about anything right now. Joy feels good, but wrong.*

*Frustrating. Confusing. Weird.*

---

If we're honest, most of us see ourselves as the center of the universe. We don't say that, but we think and act that way. We view life through the lens of self.

This greatly colors and perhaps even determines how we see

hardship, loss, and emotional pain. We don't like it, therefore it's bad and to be avoided. If we're uncomfortable, we think something is wrong. We tend to see God and His love through the lens of self too. No wonder we're confused, frustrated, and even angry.

God encourages us to change our lenses. He longs for us to see things as they are. As we make Him, His love, and His Word our lens, our perspective begins to change. We begin to get the message that life involves us, but it's not about us.

The universe is designed to reveal Jesus Christ. He lives in you. He wants to be your lens, your life.

You're enduring a terrible loss. Be real with your Lord about what's happening in your heart. He loves you.

---

*For in Him all things were created: things in heaven and on earth, visible and invisible, whether thrones or powers or rulers or authorities; all things have been created through Him and for Him. He is before all things, and in Him all things hold together.*
*Colossians 1:16-17*

*I embrace the truth that life is about You. Everything owes its existence to You. You are the center and focus. Lord, You are my life. Be my center and my focus.*

# 123

*My spouse's birthday is coming up.*
*What am I going to do?*

*I can't celebrate, can I? Wouldn't that be wrong,*
*irreverent, disrespectful or something?*

*It hurts to even think about this. I would rather*
*the day just disappear from the calendar.*

*I'm smart enough to know that sitting around*
*and dreading the day's relentless approach*
*isn't going to do me or anyone else any good.*
*Yet, I'm clueless. I feel a little paralyzed.*

*I can feel the grief welling up inside me. The pressure*
*is building as their special day comes. How do I*
*celebrate the day they were born when they're dead?*

---

Birthdays are special indeed. Your spouse's birthday is forever enshrined in your heart. It should be.

God thought about your spouse before He created the earth and the world. He determined the time and place where they would be born and live. He personally knit them together in the womb. The day of their birth was clearly written on His divine calendar. It was a special day indeed when your life partner - a unique, created-in-God's-image, one-of-a-kind individual of priceless, eternal value - took their first breath.

Use the day to honor them. Make a simple plan that involves remembering them. Light a candle in their honor. Give a donation in their name. Buy a card and write to them. Set up an empty chair and tell them what you miss. Write to God, telling Him what you miss and how you feel.

Speak their name out loud and talk about them to someone. Go through a photo album, thanking God for them and all they were and are to you. Have a simple gathering and invite others to share and tell stories.

I know all this might sound emotional and scary. Remembering our loved ones and celebrating their lives brings healing to our hearts.

Let God be the focus of your remembering. This helps put loss, death, grief, and life in perspective.

*You discern my going out and my lying down; you are familiar with all my ways. Before a word is on my tongue you, Lord, know it completely.*
*Psalm 139:3-4*

*Lord, You know me. You know my heart and my grief. Be my comfort. Make this birthday count. Use it to bring healing and hope to my shaky soul.*

# 124

*Thinking about my spouse's birthday triggered more fears about other days lurking ahead on the calendar. Thanksgiving. Christmas. Valentine's Day. And the anniversary of their death.*

*I feel like the Grinch. I want to stop these days from coming.*

*I need to change my attitude somehow. It does no good to hunker down in dread. I want to turn this around and use these days to help me grieve and heal.*

*Surely, these times can be part of God's plan for me and those around me. I can't yet imagine it, but I'm sure He can use these days for good—for everyone who knew and cared about my spouse.*

---

Yes, He can. He will. These days are special to Him too. He knows them well. He knows your heart and mind and all you're grappling with as time moves on. He feels your grief and pain.

He wants to use these special times to express His love for you. Birthdays, holidays, and anniversaries can be hard. We love. We experience heavy loss. We grieve. We heal as we remember and continue to express our love, trusting God as we travel this path of grief.

As special days approach, deal with the dread and anxiety by taking action. Make a simple plan. Intentionally honor your spouse. Involve others if possible. Talk about your partner, share, and celebrate their lives.

These holidays and special seasons will be forever different now, but they can still be good. Keep sharing with God what's happening inside you. He loves you. He will guide you through this.

———◆———

*Love always protects, always trusts, always hopes, always perseveres. Love never fails.*
*1 Corinthians 13:7-8*

*Love endures. Lord, express your love through me on these special days. Reassure me and heal me. I will trust You by making simple plans to love and honor my loved one.*

# 125

*My spouse's birthday was better than I expected.*

*I woke up nervous. I was anxious all morning.*
*I set up a picture and then placed the card*
*I bought for them in front of it.*

*In the card, I placed a letter I wrote, detailing*
*what I miss. I didn't edit. I simply wrote*
*what I was thinking and feeling.*

*I read the letter out loud. It was hard. It was*
*emotional. But it was good. I felt relieved afterward.*

*Later we gathered as a family and some others came*
*over too. I asked everyone to get a birthday card and*
*write in it whatever they wanted. We opened cards*
*one by one and people read what they wrote.*

*It was hard, but delightful. We got to grieve together.*
*And I was able to grieve on my own too.*

*It turned out to be a good day.*

---

I'm proud of you. You were intentional. You made a plan. You
expressed your grief and what was happening inside you. You
involved others. You gave them a tremendous gift by inviting
them to grieve with you.

You remembered your spouse. You celebrated their life. You spoke their name and shared their story. You honored them on their birthday. That took courage and faith. Well done.

As we honor those the Lord has placed in our lives, we honor Him. We acknowledge Him as the planner and creator of the universe, ourselves, and all those we care about and love. We acknowledge that we are created in His image and designed for relationship.

When we remember, we also look ahead to the great reunion that is still in front of us. It will be a wonderful day indeed. We lean forward into eternity a little more. Our hearts remind us that this world is not our ultimate home.

———◆———

*Since you call on a Father who judges each person's work impartially, live out your time as foreigners here in reverent fear.*
*1 Peter 1:17*

*You thought of me and planned me long before I was born. I am not from here. I am from You. This world is not my home. You are my home. Give me eternal perspective, Lord.*

# 126

*I'm thankful my spouse's birthday went well.*
*It was emotional and draining. I'm exhausted,*
*but it's a good kind of exhaustion. I honored*
*them and expressed my love. That felt good.*

*I'm more hopeful now about the other special days*
*ahead—Thanksgiving, Christmas, and my mate's*
*death anniversary. I'm going to make a plan, involve*
*other people, and honor them as much as possible.*

*Love doesn't die. I knew that intellectually, but I know*
*it in my heart. I still love my spouse. I always will. I can*
*still express that, even though they're not here with me.*

*I want to give God His place in all this. Without Him,*
*my spouse would never have been here, and neither*
*would I. He is good. Life and love are gifts from Him.*

---

Much of our angst about grief has to do with the unknown. We don't know what's coming next, how things will work out, or who we will be on the other side of this time of pain and loss. Being able to be proactive and plan for holidays and special times feels good. We're taking steps and making decisions to grieve well.

You're right. Love doesn't die. We're created in God's image. We are eternal people. In our basic identity, we are spirits who have souls, housed in bodies. This life is just the beginning, the preface, the introduction.

When we love, we honor Him who is love. When we honor our spouses, we honor the One who thought of them, planned them, created them and placed them in our lives.

Fundamentally, our lives are about Him. His plan involves us, but it's not about us. When we choose to place Him first, life begins to make more sense.

⸻ ❖ ⸻

*Many are the plans in a person's heart, but it is the Lord's purpose that prevails.*
*Proverbs 19:21*

*Lord, You are life. You are my life. Your will be done in my life as it is in heaven. My life is ultimately about You.*

# 127

*This morning I realized that my heart had turned a corner. I had been thinking and acting like a victim. I saw all this as something that happened to me. I think somewhere deep inside, I blamed God.*

*I reasoned, "He could have stopped it. This didn't have to happen. Why did He take my spouse?"*

*Rationally, I know that God doesn't cause all things. That would make Him the author of evil and suffering. We live in a broken, wounded world where unspeakable and painful things happen. Why us? Why them? Why me? Why then? These questions are too big for me, but my heart churned on them incessantly.*

*I have to come to the point of accepting what I can't understand. Otherwise, I commit myself to a life of anger, frustration, guilt, and more pain. It's not so much what happened, but how I see it and what I do with it that seems to matter most now.*

---

The lenses we look through make all the difference. We see tragedy. We experience pain, suffering, and deep loss. We can lose ourselves in asking, "Where is God in all this?"

With the lens of faith, we don't ignore this question, but we choose to see the world more as God does. We live in a broken place full of challenges, loss, anxiety, and fear. Amid this bleak environment, God is at work expressing His love and care. He is busy bringing hope, healing, and triumphant good out of disaster.

Little-known parts of the Serenity Prayer come to mind: "Living one day at a time, enjoying one moment at a time; accepting hardship as a pathway to peace; taking, as Jesus did, this sinful world as it is, not as I would have it; trusting that You will make all things right..."

We are heading to a place where everything is as it should be. This world, however, is not that place. God offers us His companionship and peace amid the present turmoil. He makes all the difference.

---

*My heart is not proud, Lord, my eyes are not haughty; I do not concern myself with great matters or things too wonderful for me. But I have calmed and quieted myself, I am like a weaned child with its mother; like a weaned child I am content.*
**Psalm 131:1-3**

*Lord, renew me and transform my thinking. Give me more of an eternal perspective. Speak to me. I rest in You. You are my life.*

# 128

*Well, I got the aren't-you-over-this-yet eye roll yesterday.*

*Actually, I've gotten that a lot. I decided to talk about my spouse, even if others were reluctant to bring them up. Hardly anyone mentions them. Instead of waiting to hear their name from others' lips, I decided to start speaking it myself.*

*Thankfully, some people have responded well. I find that if I share positively, rather than simply emoting, people are more able to listen and take it in. A few of them have joined in and shared about their loved ones who have died.*

*But I still get those eye rolls sometimes. Oh well. I guess that's inevitable. I'm trying not to take it personally and remember that their reaction is about them and not about me or my spouse.*

---

Most people are compassionate and will give us a chance to grieve—for a while. Then, they expect us to be back to normal. By normal, I mean back to the way we were before. Of course, that's impossible. We're not the same people anymore.

If we were the same, what would that say about our spouse? What would that say about us and our hearts?

When we encounter a massive loss like this, we struggle. We grieve. Over time, we adjust, heal, and grow. We're not the same as before, and we shouldn't be.

I'm glad you've decided to grieve well, speak your spouse's name, talk about them, and let the chips fall where they may. You've discovered a key truth. When we share positively—things like good memories and pleasant stories—people tend to respond better. Many times, your sharing will encourage them to share about their losses. This is healing for everyone.

As you honor God with your grief and sharing, you'll sense His companionship and blessing. He is empowering you to grieve well and live well.

———◆———

*Shout for joy, you heavens; rejoice, you earth; burst into song, you mountains! For the Lord comforts His people and will have compassion on His afflicted ones.*
*Isaiah 49:13*

*You are my life, Lord. I can do nothing apart from you. Continue to comfort me. Help me to grieve well. Use my grief for your plans and purposes.*

# 129

*Certain things have become special to
me. Photos. Objects. Places. Things that
remind me of my love, my spouse.*

*Some of these things were special before, but
now they've taken on a whole new significance.
When I see them, I remember. And when I
remember, I feel the grief and the gratitude.*

*My spouse isn't with me here anymore, but I'm
thankful for them – their companionship and love.
They were, and are, a gift to me. God personally
created my spouse. He made all this possible.*

*At first, these reminders brought pain to my heart.
Now, they bring a new kind of joy. It feels different.
Memories are tinged with grief and sadness, but
also brimming with thankfulness and gratitude.*

*I'm so glad my spouse was in my life, and I in theirs.
I'm glad we were one. I'm hurting, but I'm blessed.*

———◆———

When our spouse departs, the loss takes over our hearts for a
while. All we can feel is the grief and the pain. We're shocked
and stunned. Life has changed. The world has changed.

As we openly express our hearts to God and share with Him

what's happening inside us, we begin to sense His presence with us. We experience His love amid the pain, sadness, anger, and confusion. Over time, He heals our wounded hearts.

This doesn't mean we stop grieving or missing our spouse. We may always grieve on some level. But the grief is changing. As we allow God to renew our minds while we're hurting, we begin to see things with more perspective. Gratitude for our life partner and all we experienced with them grows and begins to exert its influence in our hearts.

We find memorials around us—things that remind us of our spouse and evoke fond memories. These pictures, objects, or places become even more special to us.

We remember. We thank God for our spouses.

---

*"The Lord is my strength and my defense; He has become my salvation. He is my God, and I will praise Him, my father's God, and I will exalt Him."*
*Exodus 15:2*

*You have blessed me, Lord. I'm grateful for those You have placed in my life. I will praise You, for You created them and brought our paths together. I will exalt You.*

# 130

*At first, memories brought only pain and sadness.*
*Now, they bring mostly gratitude and smiles.*

*I don't know when this change took place. It happened*
*over time, bit by bit. I didn't realize it at first. Then*
*one day, I felt different. My smile had returned. I*
*realized I felt some joy somewhere deep inside.*

*I'm not saying that I'm all better or that I'm*
*past losing my spouse. I've learned enough to*
*never say that I'm done grieving. I'll always miss*
*them. I love them. My grief will continue.*

*But that grief is changing. The color is seeping back*
*into life, little by little, day by day. At first, I felt guilty*
*feeling anything good. Now I realize that joy is a gift,*
*and I honor my spouse when I allow myself to feel it.*

*Like grief, joy can be a way I remember them.*
*They brought much joy to me, so when I think*
*of them, feeling joyful is natural. It's a mixed*
*bag—a mysterious combo of grief and gladness.*

---

Grief and life are certainly a mixed bag. So much variety. So many unexpected twists and turns. So many good things combined with so much tragedy. The ups and downs are extraordinary, and many of them can leave us breathless.

You're describing a healthy grief process. We feel the terrible loss. Sadness, anger, confusion, frustration, and emotional pain ensue. Our emotions are all over the place. It takes a toll on us mentally, physically, and even spiritually as well. Our spouse, our life partner, is no longer here, and the change is stunning and shocking.

Our hearts take time to adjust. We grieve. We long for them. We hunger for their presence, their voice, and their touch. We miss them and everything about them. The loss permeates all of life.

Then one day a shift occurs. It's been happening over time, but we haven't noticed. We feel different. Our grief has changed. Our new terrain is growing more familiar somehow. God is healing us.

And He will continue to heal you. He is faithful. He is committed to you. He bathes your wounds in His love.

---

*They will enter Zion with singing; everlasting joy will crown their heads. Gladness and joy will overtake them, and sorrow and sighing will flee away.*
*Isaiah 35:10*

*You can turn disaster into blessing. Thank you for bringing gladness and joy back into my life and heart. You are my Healer. I praise You.*

# 131

*Just when I think I'm healing, I have another grief burst.*

*Yesterday's burst was a big one. It came out of nowhere.
I couldn't even identify a trigger. I felt terribly
sad. Emotion welled up and spilled out of me.*

*Afterwards, I felt better, but also embarrassed.
I felt like I had done something wrong or gone
backwards somehow. I felt like a failure.*

*I thought, "Great. I can't even do grief
right. Where did I go wrong? What is this?"
I'm trying to accept myself in this.*

*I know I need to be patient with myself,
but this feels like such a setback.*

*I miss my spouse terribly. I would give
almost anything for one more embrace.*

---

Grief has no timetable. Grief bursts can come at any time, anywhere, with any intensity, at any stage of our grief process.

When can we honestly say our grief process is done? We know intellectually that we'll always grieve on some level because we'll always miss our spouses. We're surrounded by reminders, so feeling sadness again isn't surprising.

Yet our hearts want to be past the pain of this terrible loss. Deep down, we want to honor our spouses and the Lord with joy and gratitude. We want to live well and allow God to live through us to make a difference in the world around us. Sometimes grief bursts can seem like an enemy trying to scuttle our growth and progress.

Grief bursts are actually more like a broken bone. If we break our leg, we're not surprised at soreness from time to time with sudden weather shifts or more than usual exertion. Our leg healed, but it is not the same.

Our hearts are healing, but they are not the same. Grief bursts will come. Ride them out. Feel the grief. Be present as much as possible in the moment. The Lord is with you. His arms are around you. Rest in Him.

---

*My eyes are ever on the Lord, for only He*
*will release my feet from the snare.*
*Psalm 25:15*

*Lord, I give my emotions and all future grief bursts to*
*You. Encourage me and remind me that these times*
*are part of your healing process. My eyes are on You.*

# 132

*I'm hard on myself. I expect ridiculous things of my*
*body, mind, and heart. I guess I think I'm superhuman.*

*I feel sad, and I judge myself. I talk to myself*
*and try to move out of the sadness into something*
*more pleasant. I pray. I repeat Scriptures*
*that come to mind. I distract myself.*

*It's like I've spilled a drink. I'm embarrassed and*
*irritated with myself. I sigh and rush around trying*
*to wipe it up so there's no trace of the spill remaining.*
*I want my life neat, clean, and mistake free.*

*How unrealistic is that?*

*Every time I think I'm doing better, something*
*happens. I feel derailed. I'm disappointed with*
*myself and frustrated with circumstances.*

*The loss of my spouse, my love, has changed everything.*

---

Most of us tend to be hard on ourselves in some way. We want
to feel competent and somewhat in control of our thoughts,
feelings, and behavior. As grief goes on, we get used to some
things, but get irritated with others. After feeling out of control
about everything, we're hungry to have some ability to manage
what happens in us and around us.

We have ideas in our head about how grief should go. When it doesn't pan out that way, we look in the mirror. We judge ourselves. We're blowing it somehow.

Of course, we know our expectations are unrealistic. Many times, we live according to what we want to be true rather than what really is. We want to be past the unpleasantness of grief.

We live from our hearts. Our spouse is gone, and our hearts have been wounded. These wounds get bumped in life, and we feel pain all over again. Nothing is wrong. This is natural and healthy. God heals our wounds, but His healing process isn't about taking our wounds away. He uses our losses (yes, even this loss) to grow and mature us—to deepen our love for Him and trust in Him.

He never wastes pain. He uses your grief for your good.

---

*The Lord upholds all who fall*
*and lifts up all who are bowed down.*
*Psalm 145:14*

*No matter how I feel or what happens, You are with me. You are in me, and I am in You. Heal my heart. Use my wounds for good. Deepen my love for You.*

# 133

*I thank God for the people in my life who know
grief, especially those who have lost spouses. They
make such a difference. They care. They listen.
They don't judge. They support. They get it.*

*I'm learning to listen and serve by watching and
interacting with them. Just being in their presence brings
me a great sense of safety. Somehow, I know everything
is going to be okay, even if it doesn't feel that way.*

*These people are gifts from God. I want to
be a gift to others too. I pray for the patience
and love to see people and to listen.*

*I knew listening was important. Now, I
know it's one of life's most important skills.
Listening is a huge part of love.*

---

Jesus loved us by entering our worlds and walking with us
in our mess. He loved us by giving Himself for us. When we
put aside our agendas, see others, and take time to enter their
world, amazing things can happen. This is love in action.

Spending time with loving, caring, and inspiring people has a
great impact. Our hearts naturally respond. We're created to
love God and love people, and when we're with others who are
doing that our hearts come alive in new ways.

God puts these people in our lives. Jesus gave His life for us so that He could give His life to us and live His life through us. These safe people are allowing that to happen. They are reflections of Jesus to those around them. When this happens, everybody wins.

Even amid the painful loss of a spouse, God is healing you. He lives in you and wants to live through you to comfort and love others. What an honor it is to be a part of what He is doing. If we're willing, our own suffering can open us up to be used by God in new and even deeper ways.

---

*There is surely a future hope for you,*
*and your hope will not be cut off.*
*Proverbs 23:18*

*Thank you for using people to remind me of your*
*goodness and faithfulness. You have a plan for me. You*
*are my hope. Let me be a hope-bringer to others.*

# 134

*The loss of my life partner has caused me to look back and review my life. I've been blessed. I've blown it many times. My life is an interesting mix of ups and downs.*

*I guess most people could say that. If I compare, I can always find someone with a better life. I can also find someone who has had it much worse. What do I know? I'm not on the inside of their lives or hearts. I only know my own.*

*I find myself thinking about forgiveness a lot. I've forgiven others. Yet, old stuff pops up, now more than ever. Do I forgive again?*

*Sometimes I find myself wondering if I need to forgive God. I've held Him responsible for things along the way, without knowing it at the time. I believe I allowed some wounds to distance me from Him. Is it weird or wrong to forgive God?*

*In any case, my heart is in forgiveness mode at present, and I want to cover as much ground as possible.*

---

The loss of a spouse can bring clarity and depth to many things, including the importance of forgiveness. Forgiveness is one of life's greatest and most practical skills. It's one of the basic ways we can care for and guard our own hearts.

We forgive as often as necessary. We forgive any time a past wound or offense comes up. We release the offense and the person, again. Often, the hardest thing is releasing ourselves by accepting God's forgiveness. Most of us carry more against ourselves than we do against anyone else. When you forgive, don't forget about releasing yourself from past errors too.

Of course, God doesn't need our forgiveness. He's perfect and never does anything that is not loving. But we don't always see it this way. We often see Him as responsible for pain—either causing or allowing it—and subconsciously we can begin to distance ourselves from Him. We trust Him, but wall off parts of our hearts at the same time.

God doesn't need us to release Him from blame, but perhaps our own hearts do. Many of us need to release our heavenly Father from blame in order to clear out some of what holds us back from intimacy with Him. Blame always hinders trust.

Releasing others (even God) from blame frees our hearts to live.

---

*Then Peter came to Jesus and asked, "Lord, how many times shall I forgive my brother or sister who sins against me? Up to seven times?" Jesus answered, "I tell you, not seven times, but seventy times seven times."*
*Matthew 18:21-22*

*Lord, I release all offenses and wrongs done to me by others. I forgive. Help me to forgive frequently and quickly in the future. You live in me. You are an expert at this.*

# 135

*I'm still thinking about forgiveness today. In fact,*
*this morning I wrote an "offense" list. I went back*
*and thought about what has happened in my life.*
*Some things I felt peaceful about, like I had already*
*dealt with those situations. Other events and*
*names triggered emotions that were unpleasant.*

*I thought about those people and forgave them— again. I*
*even forgave my spouse for leaving. I forgave them for all*
*I've missed already and all I'm going to miss in the future*
*because they're not here. I forgave and released all those*
*who disappeared during my grief process—including*
*those who were critical, judgmental, and even mean.*

*And I released God from blame—for my loved*
*one's death, for the wounds in my life, for*
*other people's behavior, and for bad things*
*that have happened along the way.*

*It felt good. I cleaned my spiritual house.*
*My heart feels lighter. I needed that.*

---

We carry much that we don't have to. Most of us are burdened
by weights from the past that we've gotten so used to carrying
that we don't notice them anymore. They're still there, however, weighing us down more than we realize.

Forgiveness is always a good, godly, and holy thing. God is an expert at it. He lives in you. When you forgive, He is working in and through you.

At some point it dawns on us that we're the ones that benefit from forgiving others. We're actually releasing ourselves. Forgiveness isn't saying it didn't matter, but that it mattered deeply—so deeply that we don't want it to scuttle our lives and relationships. When we forgive others, we set our own hearts free.

When our hearts are free, our ability to trust goes up. We have more energy to love. When we forgive, Christ is at work in us in ways we're not aware of—blessing us and all those around us.

———◆———

*Bear with each other and forgive one another if any of you has a grievance against someone. Forgive as the Lord forgave you.*
*Colossians 3:13*

*Thank you, Lord, for your forgiveness. Thank you that You live in me. Work in me to practice forgiveness. Life is heavy, and I want to travel as light as possible.*

# 136

*I have so many memories. As I look back, the
guilt and regret surfaces. I tend to ruminate on
that. I can venture into dark places quickly. I'm
naturally hard on myself, even about the past.*

*I hold myself hostage. I know this holds me back. I
know this doesn't benefit me or anyone else. Guilt
doesn't help me grieve, and it certainly doesn't help my
relationship with God. Yet, I seem to give in to it quickly.*

*Do I want to punish myself somehow? When I think of
the death of my spouse, the what-if's come barreling
into my mind and heart. I've been over this ground
dozens of times. Will I ever be done with guilt?*

*Guilt is not my friend. I must guard my heart.
Sometimes I seem especially vulnerable to guilt's voice.*

---

Guilt can be nasty. It is persistent, persuasive, and unforgiving. It keeps coming, knocking, and intruding. Guilt can exert powerful influence in our minds and hearts.

Try not to focus on the guilt. Focus gives guilt exactly what it wants—your attention and energy. It wants you all to itself. Guilt is an expert at distraction and discouragement.

Shift your heart from guilt to God's forgiveness. What Christ did for you on the cross was completely effective. All your sin has been paid for and your guilt wiped out. The ledger is clean. There is now no condemnation for you.

Let that sink in. No condemnation. Christ took it all. He has granted you His freedom. You are a new creation now.

Keep releasing the past. Ask God to remind you that you are forgiven and free.

---

*Therefore, there is now no condemnation for those who are in Christ Jesus.*
**Romans 8:1**

*Lord, let me experience and live the freedom that I have in You. Reassure me of your love and forgiveness. Empower me to release all that is not helpful in following You.*

# 137

*I want to put my grief to work. I want to use it
to honor my spouse, my life partner. I want all
the pain, confusion, and frustration to count.*

*I want to be a better listener. I want to look into
others' eyes and hear more of their hearts. I want
God to use me to bring comfort and hope.*

*I've been comforted in all this—even when the
grief was intense. I couldn't see it then, but I
can now. God's fingerprints are everywhere. He
is loving me, protecting me, guiding me.*

*I'm still grieving, but I want to give back.
I've been thinking about serving somehow in
my support group. Perhaps that's a start.*

---

When we choose to use our grief for fuel, everyone benefits.
Our own hearts take a leap of healing. We get out of our own
heads and connect with others. We exercise our wounded
hearts.

God comforts us in all our troubles. There may be times when
we don't feel this, but that doesn't change the fact that He is
with us, loving us and guiding us.

We can't give away what we don't have, but once we receive

God's love and comfort amid pain and loss, it begins to grow in us and eventually spills out of us to those around us. When we serve, we heal a little more.

So much of life is about overcoming. Jesus has overcome the world, and He lives in you. He invites you to be a conduit of His life and love to a hurting world.

Wounded hearts can grow either bitter or compassionate. God uses compassionate, humble hearts to change the world, one soul at a time.

---

*This is to my Father's glory, that you bear much fruit, showing yourselves to be my disciples.*
**John 15:8**

*Produce your fruit in me, Lord. Work through me. Love others through me, even while I'm hurting. Use me to bring hope and healing.*

# 138

*I realized something this morning. The Lord was*
*with my spouse when they died. He was there.*
*He was with them in the moment. I believe He*
*was loving them in ways that I cannot know.*

*I don't pretend to understand this. I believe that*
*God is everywhere and that He is loving. He was*
*there. He was somehow expressing His love.*

*They say we all die alone. I guess that's true in*
*a sense. But in another way, we're never alone.*
*I choose to believe that the Lord, who loves us,*
*is especially close when death approaches.*

*My mind doesn't get it, but my heart somehow*
*does. The Lord is my comfort. He is love.*

---

God works in ways that we do not see and many times cannot
understand. He has perspective that we do not. He knows all
things. He is perfect in His wisdom and His love.

Yes, He was with your spouse in that moment, just as He is
here, now. In certain traumatic or even evil situations, this is
hard to imagine. I too think that God is especially close in
times of pain, danger, and death.

It is easy to forget that He has been through this Himself.

There are many traumatic deaths, but none can top what Jesus went through. False accusations, hatred, abuse, betrayal, rejection, beating, and torture, all leading up to a slow and excruciatingly painful death while hanging near naked and exposed for all to see.

He knows. No matter what the situation, He gets it. Yes, He was with your spouse. He is with us. He is our ultimate friend and confidant.

Even when we don't understand, we can trust. This is part of what it means to walk in faith.

————◆————

*Do not be anxious about anything, but in every situation, by prayer and petition, with thanksgiving, present your requests to God. And the peace of God, which transcends all understanding, will guard your hearts and your minds in Christ Jesus.*
*Philippians 4:6-7*

*You are my constant companion, Lord. You are faithful, even when I am not. I want intimate fellowship with You. You are with me. You are in me. I love You.*

# 139

*I think I have been chasing perfection all my life.*

*I want life to be smooth, beautiful, and delightful.
I want my work to be productive and yield good,
beneficial results. I want to live without aging.
I want everything to be good all the time.*

*Sounds ridiculous, but deep down that must be what I
want. When it's not that way, I get irritated and upset.
No wonder I've struggled with losing my spouse.*

*On the one hand, I've never wanted to settle for mediocre
or anything less than good. On the other hand, I seem to
have trouble accepting and dealing with things as they
are. I'm always trying to change whatever I don't like.*

*Perhaps I need to accept what I cannot change and
focus on loving those around me. I want to trust the
Lord, but sometimes I'm not sure what that looks like.*

---

Most of us try to control situations and people to get what we
think we need or what we want. We come out of the womb
trying to make life work for us. We often do this without
God—or at best with God on the periphery.

We think of this as our life. We ask God to bless us and our plans. We feel betrayed by Him when trouble, pain, or loss invades. We seek comfort. We like smooth and easy.

God invites us to something better. He invites us to experience Him and trust Him amid all the pain and frustration of life. We're continually confronted by the reality that, while we might have influence, we control next to nothing and anything can happen at any time to anyone.

This is not our life. Life is a gift from Him. It's not about us or our comfort. It's about Him and His plan for crushing evil and being with us forever.

He is life. Life is about Him. He lives in you. You are living His life today. This is His story, and you are a part of it.

———◆———

*For in Christ all the fullness of the Deity lives in bodily form, and in Christ you have been brought to fullness.*
*Colossians 2:9-10*

*I have You, Lord. Therefore, I have everything. This is your story. Thank you for including me. I want to know You better. You are life.*

# 140

*Perhaps in my pursuit of my own little Garden of Eden,
I'm actually longing for heaven. Is that possible?*

*Now that I've lost my spouse, I look around me and ask
the question, "Is this all there is?" Loss will do that to
a person. I'm thinking about things more deeply now.*

*This is not all there is. It can't be. God says it isn't. There
is so much more. There is a spiritual reality all around
me that I can't see. Things are not simply as they appear.*

*I wonder what heaven is like. I know
it's good. Better than good.*

*Perhaps heaven is here, all around me, in some
way. I don't know. My eyesight is so limited.*

❖

We all long for heaven in many ways. We yearn to be loved and
accepted as we are. We long to be fully ourselves. We hunger to
be free from things that harm, hinder, and bind us.

Most of all, deep down, we're designed to be with the One
who thought of us, wanted us, and created us. Only He truly
knows who we are.

We thirst for heaven because we long for God Himself. Our
hearts stretch to know Him, be with Him, and experience Him

without hindrance. We were created to live forever with Him in His immediate presence.

We journey through a foreign wasteland, heading home. Our hearts never feel fully at home here. We instinctively know there's something more, something greater and better.

We experience His love now. He walks with us here. He gives us glimpses of what's to come. Over time, He can set our minds more on eternal things, giving us perspective for life here and making contentment possible no matter what the circumstances.

He made us for Himself. Nothing less will satisfy our hearts.

---

*For our light and momentary troubles are achieving for us an eternal glory that far outweighs them all. So we fix our eyes not on what is seen, but on what is unseen, since what is seen is temporary, but what is unseen is eternal.*
*2 Corinthians 4:17-18*

*Lord, you made me for yourself. I belong to You. Only You can satisfy my longings. I lean into You. I worship You. I delight in You.*

# 141

*I have many questions. I'm assuming all of them will
be answered one day, but probably not in this life.*

*"Why?" is still the most pressing question. I wonder
this about a lot of things. Then again, there seems
to be a part of me that doesn't have to understand.
Perhaps this is the best part of my heart. It's learned
to be peaceful and to take things as they come.*

*I look back at all the losses. This death of my spouse
has unearthed all the previous losses and given them
life again. Life is hard. Painful. Full of joy at times,
yes, but also permeated with unwanted surprises.*

*Perhaps when I see the Lord, all my questions
will evaporate. Maybe I'll instantly know all the
answers I need. I'm certain that I'll be thrilled,
peaceful, and content all at the same time.
My angst will not enter heaven with me.*

*That will be nice. No angst. No under-the
surface grumblings and frustrations.*

Heaven will be far beyond our best expectations. We will finally be exactly who we were designed to be, and the same will
be true for everyone around us there.

I have a feeling that when we arrive in heaven our hearts will shout, "Yes! This is what I've dreamed about and longed for all my life and never knew it!" As you said, perhaps all our questions will be answered, or maybe they will simply evaporate because they don't matter anymore.

It will be a wonderful and grand reunion with all those we know and love, who know and love the Lord. I can't imagine the freedom and the unbridled joy and delight. No more sin. No more wondering. No more anxiety or fear.

He is preparing a place for us. He knows us. Only He knows who we truly are. His love is perfect. He will complete the work He started in us. He is faithful. We have much to look forward to.

———◆———

*Dear friends, now we are children of God, and what we will be has not yet been made known. But we know that when Christ appears, we shall be like Him, for we shall see Him as he is.*
*1 John 3:2*

*Lord, give me heavenly eyes. Set my mind on You. Enable me to see reality as it is. Help me to trust You. I release all my questions to You.*

# 142

*I don't sit still very well. Most of my prayers
are what I call "flare prayers." I fire them
spontaneously, here and there, during the day.*

*I don't rest well either, especially since the loss of my
love, my spouse. However, it's getting a little better
over time. I'm finding my emotional footing again.
My heart seems a little calmer and more settled.*

*I'm certainly not the same, and I never will be. I
don't want to be the same. I want to heal and grow.*

*I see things more clearly now. I control so
little. Prayer is the most powerful thing I
can do—for myself and for others.*

*I want to offer more than flare prayers. I am making
a list. There is so much to pray for. I want to take
time each day to pray. I want to pray throughout
the day. I want prayer to be my lifestyle. I want to
pray for people when I see them, while I'm talking
to them, and anytime I think about them.*

*God is certainly using others' prayers
in my life. I'm grateful.*

---

God is remarkably generous. He invited us to participate in what He is doing, even while we're missing our spouse and grieving. Prayer is a huge part of that.

Prayer isn't so much about asking for things, but rather it's a conversation with the Almighty One. We're sharing our hearts with Him. We're intentionally thinking out loud in His presence. We're being open, real, and authentic with Him.

He invites us to ask, seek, and knock. We're healthiest when we live openly with Him and pray about everything. Prayer isn't about results, but rather about companionship.

As we pray, we trust. We share our hearts with Him. We ask. We leave things in His hands. We watch to see what He will do. He is always at work, and He is certainly at work in and through our prayers.

"Pray continuously," Paul said. Prayer and trusting our Father is not a task, but a lifestyle—a continual condition of our hearts.

———◈———

*So I say to you: Ask and it will be given to you; seek and you will find; knock and the door will be opened to you. For everyone who asks receives; the one who seeks finds; and to the one who knocks, the door will be opened.*
*Luke 11:9-10*

*Remind me, Lord, that prayer is conversation with You. Give me the power to be real and share my heart with You. Speak to me. Deepen and enrich my walk with You.*

# 143

*I often wonder what to pray for. Do
others wonder about this?*

*I end up praying for the results I want—in my own
life or someone else's—and then saying something
like, "Your will be done, Lord." I pray my desires,
but I'm not sure I pray with much faith.*

*The loss of my spouse has brought me to question
this. It seems there are so many unanswered prayers.
I pray, but sometimes I wonder what's the point
if God's will is going to be done anyway.*

*Is there a way to know what God's will is?
Then I could pray with confidence and faith.
At least, I think I could. I wonder what to
pray for myself. What is His will for me?*

---

There is much we don't know, but thankfully there are things
we can know for certain. These are the things that God has
revealed to us in His word about Himself, about us, and about
life.

There are things that we know are God's will, all the time. That
we love Him and express that love with our lives. That we seek
Him and trust Him. That we allow Him to live through us to

love others. That we immerse ourselves in His word and allow His thoughts to penetrate and fill our minds and hearts.

These are things we can pray for with confidence and faith for ourselves and every person we meet. We might not know God's specific will about this or that, but we do know He longs for us to experience Him and His love amid all the trouble of this life – even after the loss of a beloved spouse.

God invites us to set our minds on heavenly things—on spiritual reality—and pray accordingly. As we do this, we see more of the larger picture.

---

*If you remain in me and my words remain in you,*
*ask whatever you wish, and it will be done for you.*
**John 15:7**

*I want to know You better, Lord. The better I*
*know You, the clearer I will discern your will.*
*I give myself again to You. You are my life.*

# 144

*Life is about a relationship with God. It must be.
Nothing else makes sense. Nothing else satisfies. The
loss of my spouse has made this clearer to me.*

*Yet, I'm amazed how quickly I can wander
from this. I get caught up in my own stuff—the
daily routine, responsibilities, and the flurry
of interruptions and unexpected obstacles.
God gets shoved to the periphery quickly.*

*Sometimes I lay my head on the pillow at night
and realize I haven't thought of Him all day. Sad.
Who knows what opportunities I've missed?*

*After this most recent death, I'm on a mission to live
life well. I want to make the most of each moment.*

---

God is patient with us. We, however, tend to be impatient with ourselves.

When we get frustrated, consider that as God's invitation to return to what we know to be true. He is real. He is sovereign and works out all things for His glory and our good. He loves us. He is perfect. He is our life. He is our home.

No matter how distracted we get, these things never change, because He never changes. On our worst day, His love for us is still perfect and His commitment to us still total. As we rest in Him and all the certainties that surround Him, our hearts relax more. Instead of holding ourselves hostage with guilt, we sigh, look to the Lord, and ask Him to continue to fill us and live through us.

It's not what happened or what we did or didn't do but what we do next that matters most now. He invites us to be still and know that He is God. He is certain. He is sure. We are learning and growing, even while enduring this deep, terrible loss. He is patient and completely committed to us.

He will complete what He has begun in us. This is certain because He is certain.

———◆———

*Because of the Lord's great love we are not consumed, for His compassions never fail. They are new every morning; great is your faithfulness.*
*Lamentations 3:22-23*

*Lord, You are my rock and my fortress. You are my provision, my strength, and my life. You are faithful. Live through me and accomplish your will today.*

# 145

*I'm skittish about relationships and companionship.*

*I find myself wondering what others are thinking.
When I'm approached by someone interested
in me, it feels good but also terrifying.*

*I've heard some horror stories from other widowed
spouses. Some have gone out with people who
are only interested in what they can get.*

*No wonder some seek companionship online.
I can see where that would feel safer. But
I hear tragic stories about that too.*

*I don't need more tragedy or upset. I need
peace and stability. I want companionship,
but I'm wondering if it's worth it.*

*(Sigh.) I don't know how to do this.*

---

Feeling more vulnerable after losing a spouse is common and natural. We feel this way because it's true. Our hearts have been broken. We are more vulnerable. We tend to become more susceptible to things that promise relief from the loneliness inside us.

In our current state, however, the last thing we need is to feel used.

Guard your heart. Sometimes that might mean holding back. Other times it could mean launching out a bit. When in doubt, wait. Breathe deeply. Pray. Seek the Lord and His wisdom.

He has a plan for you – a good plan. He knows your needs. He is at work. As you cooperate with Him and yield to Him, He will make His path for you clear over time.

Impulsive decisions made to quell the raging loneliness within rarely work out well. Give God time.

God always meets you where you are. He invites you to rest in Him and enjoy His companionship. He will provide other companions in His time and in His way.

———

*Blessed are those who hunger and thirst for righteousness, for they will be satisfied.*
*Matthew 5:6*

*Lord, I accept the fact that I'm lonely. You are with me. You share my loneliness. Satisfy my soul in You.*

# 146

*I'm asking God to use this pain—the loss of my*
*precious spouse—for good. Along with that, I'm*
*asking Him to use all past pain for good too.*

*I can look back and see Him doing that. I can also*
*see it in this case, but not so clearly yet. I guess*
*I need time and distance to discern more. He is*
*always doing more than I can see or know.*

*I choose to believe that He is good, no matter how*
*things appear. I put aside my fickle judgments*
*based on my shortsighted, human view of*
*things. I choose to trust and rest in Him.*

*Use the pain, Lord. Use the losses, the*
*emotions, the confusion, and all the changes.*
*Heal me. Heal others. Use me.*

---

God is a master at turning tragedy and pain into good. He is
the ultimate turnaround artist.

He is always at work, loving us and loving others through us.
He is always taking what happens and turning it around and
using it to accomplish His will.

As we've said before, He never wastes pain. He speaks to us in our distress. He heals broken, wounded hearts. He enters our messes with us. He walks with us in our grief and confusion.

He uses wounded, imperfect people who are willing. He uses us even when we're unaware. He is always at work in us—speaking to our hearts, comforting us, and bringing hope. He gives peace, even in the direst circumstances.

Trust is a choice, as you said. We choose to trust now, in this moment, and then in the next moment. We contemplate His limitless love that He continually lavishes on us. We rest.

---

*It is God who arms me with strength and keeps my way secure. He makes my feet like the feet of a deer; He causes me to stand on the heights.*
*2 Samuel 22:33-34*

*You know me, Lord. Use me. Use all my weaknesses and failures for good. Turn everything around and use it for your purposes. Rivet my attention on You.*

# 147

*I accept the truth that God is loving. More than
that, I accept the truth that He loves us.*

*"For God so loved the world..." I used to think He
had to love me because I was part of the package
deal. He had to love everyone, so He loved me too.*

*It's stunning to think that the Creator of the universe—
the One who sustains everything—loves me, individually
and personally. He knows me. He knows my heart,
my mind. He thought of me, wanted me, and created
me. He died for me and rose from the dead for me.*

*For all us, yes. But also for me.*

*As I grieve, I will remember that God loves me.
He is at work. He somehow works out all things
for my good, even through the terrible pain of
losing my life partner. I will trust Him.*

---

In the book of Ephesians, Paul prays that believers might know
the love of Christ that surpasses all knowledge. The word know
here goes beyond head knowledge to personal experience. Paul
prays that we might continually experience the never-ending,
measureless, limitless love of Christ.

If we know we're completely and totally loved, it makes a massive difference in our hearts and lives. When we realize that God is not fickle, and that there is nothing we can do to cause Him to love us any more or any less, our lives turn from worry and fear to gratitude and trust. Peace invades. Joy wells up within.

We are perfectly loved by a perfect God who always loves perfectly. He is love. He is the very definition of goodness, care, compassion, and unconditional commitment. Once we trust in Christ, He lives in us and we in Him. We are now one spirit with Him. Relationship doesn't get any closer than that.

Our experience lags far behind the reality. The truth is almost too good to believe. But believe it we do. We receive. He is love. He loves us.

---

*But whoever is united with the*
*Lord is one spirit with Him.*
*1 Corinthians 6:17*

*I am in You. You are in me. I am one spirit with You. I am stunned by your goodness and love. Let me experience more of your love with each passing day.*

# 148

*I'm asking God to use the loss of my spouse and all
the pain for good somehow. I'm setting my mind
to do the same. I'm looking for ways to serve.*

*I know I'm still vulnerable. I guess I'm always
vulnerable. God says He shows Himself in and
through my weaknesses. If He uses me when I'm
like this, it's certainly not me doing it. It's Him.*

*I believe that as I serve, I will be blessed and continue to
heal. I don't want to serve to get, however, but to give.
I want to be a pipeline of God's love and compassion to
others. As I give, I receive. I'm receiving all the time.*

*I'm fatigued and sometimes exhausted. I need
balance and wisdom. I trust that God will give me
these. I will lean into Him and let Him lead.*

——————◆——————

God will bring service opportunities to you. In fact, He probably already has. And yes, He uses us greatly in times of personal weakness. The fact is that we're all weak. When we reach out to others in our weakness, they respond. They know we get it. We understand.

Most people are tired, frustrated, worried, and afraid. Few will admit this, of course. We're good at wearing our masks and playing our roles. Underneath the mask, however, many of us are screaming for hope, peace, and love.

As we receive God's love, it naturally begins to spill out of us and onto those around us. As we trust Him, it opens up pathways for Him to declare His love and care through us. He is the light. He shines through us—his cracked pots.

Broken, but healing. Wounded, yet loving. Scared at times, yet hopeful. Willing to trust and to be used for good. That's us.

---

*Therefore, my dear brothers and sisters, stand firm. Let nothing move you. Always give yourselves fully to the work of the Lord, because you know that your labor in the Lord is not in vain.*
*1 Corinthians 15:58*

*Knowing You, Lord, is my goal and my desire.*
*This is the priority of my life. You are my life.*
*Light of the world, shine through me.*

# 149

*I'm wondering if I'm ready for
companionship or even dating.*

*I still miss my spouse - terribly. Yet, my heart
feels more settled. I will never forget them,
but they are gone now, and I'm still here.*

*Living life is to be in good relationships. My
loving life partner taught me that. I want to
experience safe, loving companionship again.*

*I choose to believe God is good, and that He has good
out there for me. My heart is leaning forward, but
my head warns me to go slow and take my time.*

*My heart still aches for my spouse, but
I also want to be loved again.*

*Help me, Lord. This is all so strange.*

---

Many widowed spouses wonder when they'll be ready to consider companionship or dating. Some may never date again,
and that's okay. We're all unique with somewhat different
mindsets and values.

The key is to be yourself – who God made you – as much as
possible.

When you contemplate dating, guilt might surface. This is natural. Our hearts wonder if we're being unfaithful somehow. What God gave you with your spouse was special and unique. You can't duplicate it – nor would you want to. Every relationship is different, with two one-of-a-kind people involved.

Even if you're thinking of casual companionship, being on the same wavelength spiritually is huge. Availability and attraction aren't enough. The Bible describes us as spiritual beings currently housed in these physical bodies. Let your relationship with God be the foundation for any companionship you pursue.

God has a plan for you. Set your mind and heart on Him. Trust Him. He will direct your steps.

———⬥———

*Look to the Lord and his*
*strength; seek his face always.*
**Psalm 105:4**

*Lord, I want what You want for me. I want companionship, but I want it to flow out of my relationship with You. I belong to You.*

# 150

*I'm trying to trust, but things seem dark some days. There are times when my emotions get the better of me. Sadness takes over. Questions swirl in my mind. A tinge of hopelessness comes out of nowhere and colors everything. I miss my love, my spouse.*

*I try to ignore all this and chase it away somehow. I feel like I'm being invaded, and I fight against it. I end up stuffing the sadness to keep my mask in place.*

*It feels like I'm hiding. I want to be over this somehow. I want to feel better. I'm tired of sadness. Why does life have to be so heavy and lonely?*

*Am I doing something wrong? Have I missed something? Shouldn't I be better by now?*

*Breathe. Slow down and breathe.*

---

We're certainly in a battle. Grief, however, is not something to be fought. It is not the enemy. Grief is the natural and healthy response to a loss, especially the loss of a spouse.

If we ignore and stuff our emotions, we give them more power over us. We store them away to work secretly inside us, spreading their influence in less-than-obvious ways. The more we stuff our feelings, the more they will leak out, often in un-healthy ways.

Grief will be expressed, one way or another. It's better to acknowledge the emotions when they hit. Go ahead and feel them, as much as you can. Process them by talking, writing, or drawing. Feel them through, so that your body and mind can release them.

God isn't threatened by our emotions. He isn't shocked by our feelings. He doesn't take a step back, roll His eyes, and say, "Now, now. Get that under control."

Instead, He simply invites us to be real with Him and share what's happening inside us. The more we do this, the safer we feel. The safer we feel, the more we tend to trust. The more we trust, the more peace we have. The more peace we have, the more we heal and grow.

---

*You, Lord, are my lamp; the Lord turns*
*my darkness into light.*
*2 Samuel 22:29*

*Enable me to rest in You, Lord. You accept*
*me as I am. You love me. You are my safety*
*and security. You are my peace.*

# 151

*I don't know how many times I have to experience
it to get it. Grief is not a straight road. It's
not a clear, smooth path. It's a meandering,
obstacle-ridden, can-hardly-see-in-front-of-you
path through a thick forest laden with fog.*

*As I heal, I'm still surprised by emotion at times.
Grief sneaks up on me. Healing is an up-and-down
process. Life isn't smooth. I keep telling myself this.*

*I'm to the point where I don't like surprises much.
Lately, most of the big surprises haven't been
good. I want stability and predictability. Yet, as
I write that, I know I have stability in the Lord.
He is sure and certain. I must rest in Him.*

*The loss of my spouse has been harder than I would
have ever dreamed. I've had plenty of loss in the past,
so you would think I would know all this by now. I
guess I'm still learning. Maybe I'm just human.*

*I'm healing and growing. God is good. He
loves me. He carries me through.*

❦

We try to prepare ourselves for what's coming, even though we
don't know what that is. After the traumatic loss of a spouse,
we don't want to be surprised again by more loss and pain.

Even subconsciously, we begin constructing life to protect ourselves and those we love. We worry. We fret. Our minds spin. We live on the edge of our seats, waiting for the next unwanted hit.

On top of this, life bumps our wounds. Grief from past losses can suddenly surface again with shocking intensity. This is natural, common, and healthy. Bumped wounds should hurt.

As we walk with God through this, He teaches us. He gives us perspective, one little bit at a time. We get it intellectually, but it takes time and experience for it to trickle down into our hearts. Life is not about getting it right or never failing again. Life is about walking with God amid all the unpredictability.

He is certain. He knows. He is ordering all things for your good. He is working with all that happens and using it for His purposes. He lives in us. We live in Him. Conscious companionship with Him is what our hearts long for.

---

*For our light and momentary troubles are achieving for us an eternal glory that far outweighs them all. So we fix our eyes not on what is seen, but on what is unseen, since what is seen is temporary, but what is unseen is eternal.*
*2 Corinthians 4:17-18*

*I am a new creation. You have done this, Lord. Christ now lives in me. Companionship with You is my heart's true desire. Make me more aware of You today.*

# 152

*My perspective is changing. I can feel it.*
*The grief is changing too. I don't know*
*how to describe it. It's just different.*

*I feel different. I still miss my spouse, my life partner.*
*I always will. I still get triggered by this or that.*
*Sometimes the grief is so intense I wonder if I can*
*stand it. Yet things have settled in somehow. The loss*
*has become part of me. My spouse is a part of me.*

*My heart is still broken. At first, all I could feel was the*
*pain. I didn't know that God was there, pouring His*
*light into me. Cracks in the heart can go both ways. God*
*enables grief to pour out, while He pours Himself in.*

*I would have said that God was my constant*
*companion before, but now I have experienced this*
*in a new and deeper way. The way of pain and*
*grief can also be the path of growth and healing.*

*God says these kinds of things over and over in*
*His word. Life's bumps and bruises continually*
*challenge my heart. Am I going to live based*
*on circumstances, or what God has said?*

<hr/>

Things are not what they appear. There's always more going on than meets the eye. There are spiritual realities all around us that we cannot see. God is continually at work in ways we are unaware of.

Pain, suffering, tragedy, and death are part of this world. Our hearts rail against this, for we are eternal beings created for relationship. We are spiritual beings, with souls, housed in bodies. This world is not our home. Things happen here that are wrong, unthinkable, and even evil.

Walking with God is the only solution. It's what we were created for—to know and love Him first. When this priority is neglected, our hearts waver, our clarity wanes, and life becomes foggy.

Loss, grief, and suffering can be a pathway to peace. God uses these things to prepare us for our ultimate home and for powerful, meaningful service here. Jesus knows all about suffering, pain, and grief. He walks with us in ours. Our experience of Him grows and deepens.

---

*Do not let your hearts be troubled. You believe in God; believe also in me. My Father's house has many rooms; if that were not so, would I have told you that I am going there to prepare a place for you? And if I go and prepare a place for you, I will come back and take you to be with me that you also may be where I am.*
*John 14:1-3*

*Lord, You live in me. I live in You. I am one spirit with You. You are preparing a place for me. I am with You now. I will be with You forever. I live in certainty. You are my life.*

# 153

*I've wondered about a lot through this terrible loss.
Now, I mostly wonder about two things: What is heaven
like, and what will life be like for me here now?*

*There's no way I can know fully about either,
but I can know a little. I can know what God
has said and what He has revealed. When I don't
know something, I'll go to what I do know.*

*I know that heaven will be better than I can imagine. I
know that I will be with God face to face, without any
hindrances. I know that when I get there, everything will
make sense—or perhaps that won't even matter anymore.*

*I know that life is about walking with God,
learning from Him, experiencing Him, and
serving Him. Life is about Him. My little story
is a part of His grand story. He is my life.*

*Even while I'm grieving the loss of my spouse, life is
about choosing to trust God, moment by moment.*

God has shared about heaven with us more than we realize. He
is preparing a place for us and is preparing us for that place.
There will be no more death, crying, mourning, or pain there.
All will be life, love, peace, and joy.

We will finally be as we should be. We will be who we really are. No more relational strain or conflict. All regrets of this life will be swallowed up by grace, forgiveness, and goodness. The reunions that take place will be stunning. We will be home.

Yes, this life—all life—is about God. Life includes us, but it's not about us. He gave His life for us, so that He could give His life to us, so that He could live His life in and through us. It's all about Him, and He has included us. His goodness and love know no bounds.

This life will not be smooth or predictable. Yet, God is certain. He never changes. He is victorious over all evil, hardship, disaster, and death. We are in Him. We too are victorious. When we live out this truth, we experience His peace and joy.

He is at the center of all things. When we allow Him to occupy our hearts, we heal and grow.

---

*And I heard a loud voice from the throne saying, "Look! God's dwelling place is now among the people, and He will dwell with them. They will be His people, and God Himself will be with them and be their God. He will wipe every tear from their eyes. There will be no more death or mourning or crying or pain, for the old order of things has passed away."*
*Revelation 21:3-4*

*Lord, give me eternal perspective. Set my mind on heaven. Produce your work in and through me. Let me experience You continually.*

# 154

*I'm living on borrowed time. We all are. I look
back and am stunned at the time and energy
I've wasted on things that didn't matter.*

*My actions betrayed me. My heart was set on earthly
things—the here and now and what was happening
to me and around me. No wonder I plotted and
planned, rushed and strove. No wonder I was
derailed by each hardship, obstacle, or death.*

*I see more clearly now, and I'm grateful. I'm
slowly accepting the loss of my spouse, but I
know I'll never get over it. You don't get over a
person, especially a life partner. With God's help,
I'll get through this time of pain and grief.*

*I realize now that everything counts. Everything
matters. I want to count. I want the rest
of my days to be used for great good.*

*May your will be done, Lord, in my life as it is in
heaven. You are life. You are my life. I love you.*

---

The stakes are high. Hearts everywhere are hurting and grieving. Many have lost hope. Some had little hope to begin with. To many, life is dark.

We know the Light. Jesus said, "I am the light of the world." He also told us, "You are the light of the world." He is the Light, and He lives in us. We are light. We must shine.

We don't shine by trying. We're brightest when we trust. He shines, all the time, everywhere. He lives in us. As we walk with Him, connected with Him and centered on Him, His light naturally shines through us.

There's a fine line between trying to serve Him in our own strength and simply trusting Him to work in and through us for His good pleasure. The first option is a spiritual treadmill of effort. The second is the way of surrendered peace where we are tuned to His voice.

We make the most of the time we've been given by walking with Him, learning from Him, and trusting Him. When we do this, He lives through us and produces His fruit.

---

*For everyone born of God overcomes the world. This is the victory that has overcome the world, even our faith. Who is it that overcomes the world? Only the one who believes that Jesus is the Son of God.*
*1 John 5:4-5*

*Lord, You have overcome the world. You live in me. You have made me an overcomer. Fill me and live through me. Help me to trust You more.*

# 155

*Grief isn't for sissies. Neither is life. This is tough stuff. I'm small and limited. The Lord is up to the challenge. Nothing is impossible for Him.*

*Loss hurts. I miss my spouse. I'm going to continue to be honest about that. I'm going to look for other grieving hearts out there. I see them now. We need each other. We need compassion, understanding, and acceptance.*

*I don't know what life will be like now, but I guess I don't need to know. God knows. He is my shepherd, and He is leading. I can trust Him.*

*Sometimes I don't know exactly what trusting Him means. He will reveal it to me at the right time. Life is a step-by-step adventure with Him.*

---

When we feel seen, heard, and accepted, we feel a little safer. When we have a sense of safety, our hearts open to healing and growth. Our walls come down—not just with safe people, but with God, as well.

You are the aroma of Christ. He lives in you and wants to live through you. As you trust Him, you allow Him to do that. He reveals Himself. He touches and loves others through you.

In the process, you heal and grow as well. Everyone wins.

Christ Himself lives in you. He is an expert at grief, healing, and growth. He is perfectly compassionate, always sees things accurately, and always loves. He loves you, and nothing and no one can ever separate you from Him or His perfect love for you.

Even though your spouse is no longer here, you are safe. God is in you and surrounds you. All is well with your soul.

---

*He who was seated on the throne said, "I am making everything new!" Then He said, "Write this down, for these words are trustworthy and true." He said to me: "It is done. I am the Alpha and the Omega, the Beginning and the End. To the thirsty I will give water without cost from the spring of the water of life.*
*Revelation 21:5-6*

*Lord, I rest in You. Nurture me. Heal me. Guide me. Fill me. Use me. Live through me. I am yours.*

# Concluding Thoughts

Life is full of loss. The loss of a spouse, a life partner, is painful and even devastating.

God walks with us through this dark valley.

He comforts us, speaks to us, and guides us.

He feels what we feel.

He heals us.

He never wastes loss or pain.

He uses all that happens to us as fuel to produce eternal good in our lives and the lives of those around us.

So much of life is about overcoming.

You are an overcomer.

He lives in you. He wants to live through you.

Lean into Him. Rest. Trust.

Walk with Him.

This is His story, and you are an integral part of it.

# Topical Index

Below are some of the topics referred to in *Widowed Walk*. They are indexed by the number of the **chapter**, **not by page number**.

# An Invitation to Make a Difference

When we serve others who are hurting, our own hearts heal a little. Over time, the comfort and caring we share with those around us can add up, bringing relief and greater health to our own wounded souls.

In the latter portion of this book, we began thinking about how to use our grief to make a difference in this world and in the lives of others. If this interests you, I would like to invite you to consider becoming a part of my Difference Maker Community. As a group, we are focused on making a positive, healing impact in the lives of those around us – especially other grieving hearts.

For more information, please contact me at contact@gary-roe.com. Simply say, "I would like to know more about the Difference Maker Community," and I will respond to you personally. Together, I believe we can make a massive difference.

Warmly,
Gary

Help us reach more grieving hearts who
have lost a spouse or a loved one.
Share this link:
**https://www.garyroe.com/god-and-grief-series/**

# Additional Grief Resources

## THE COMFORT SERIES

**www.garyroe.com/comfort-series**

*Comfort for Grieving Hearts: Hope and Encouragement in Times of Loss*

*Comfort for the Grieving Spouse's Heart: Hope and Healing After Losing Your Partner*

*Comfort for the Grieving Adult Child's Heart: Hope and Healing After Losing Your Parent*

*Comfort for the Grieving Parent's Heart: Hope and Healing After Losing Your Child*

## THE GOOD GRIEF SERIES

*Aftermath: Picking Up the Pieces After a Suicide*

*www.garyroe.com/aftermath*

*Shattered: Surviving the Loss of a Child*

*www.garyroe.com/shattered*

*Teen Grief: Caring for the Grieving Teenage Heart*

*www.garyroe.com/teengrief*

*Please Be Patient, I'm Grieving: How to Care for and Support the Grieving Heart*

**www.garyroe.com/please-be-patient**

*Heartbroken: Healing from the Loss of a Spouse*

**www.garyroe.com/heartbroken-2**

*Surviving the Holidays Without You: Navigating Loss During Special Seasons*

**www.garyroe.com/surviving-the-holidays**

## THE DIFFERENCE MAKER SERIES
**www.garyroe.com/difference-maker**

*Difference Maker: Overcoming Adversity and Turning Pain into Purpose, Every Day (Adult & Teen Editions)*

*Living on the Edge: How to Fight and Win the Battle for Your Mind and Heart (Adult & Teen Editions)*

# Free On Gary's Website

## *Grief: 9 Things I Wish I had Known*

In this deeply personal and practical eBook, Gary shares nine key lessons from his own grief journeys. "This was so helpful! I saw myself on every page," said one reader. "I wish I had read this years ago," said another. Widely popular, this eBook has brought hope and comfort to thousands of grieving hearts.

Available at **www.garyroe.com**

## *The Good Grief Mini-Course*

Full of personal stories, inspirational content, and practical assignments, this 8-session email series is designed to help readers understand grief and deal with its roller-coaster emotions. Thousands have been through this course, which is now being used in support groups as well.

Available at **www.garyroe.com**.

## *The Hole in My Heart: Tackling Grief's Tough Questions*

This eBook tackles some of grief's big questions: "How did this happen?" "Why?" "Am I crazy?" "Am I normal?" "Will this get any easier?" plus others. Written in the first person, it engages and comforts the heart.

Available at **www.garyroe.com**.

## I Miss You: A Holiday Survival Kit

Thousands have downloaded this brief, easy-to-read, and very personal e-book. I Miss You provides some basic, simple tools on how to use holiday and special times to grieve well and love those around you.

Available at **www.garyroe.com**.

Help us reach other grieving hearts.

Share this link:

**https://www.garyroe.com/god-and-grief-series**

# Caring for Grieving Hearts

Visit Gary at www.garyroe.com and connect with him on Facebook, Twitter, LinkedIn, and Pinterest
Links:
Facebook: **https://www.facebook.com/garyroeauthor**
Twitter: **https://twitter.com/GaryRoeAuthor**
LinkedIn: **https://www.linkedin.com/in/garyroeauthor**
Pinterest: **https://www.pinterest.com/garyroe79/**

# About the Author

Gary's story began with a childhood of mixed messages and sexual abuse. This was followed by other losses and numerous grief experiences.

Ultimately, a painful past led Gary into a life of helping wounded people heal and grow. A former college minister, missionary in Japan, entrepreneur in Hawaii, and pastor in Texas and Washington, he now serves as a writer, speaker, chaplain, and grief counselor.

In addition to *Widowed Walk*, Gary is the author of numerous books, including the award-winning bestsellers *Shattered: Surviving the Loss of a Child*, *Comfort for the Grieving Spouse's Heart*, *Comfort for the Grieving Adult Child's Heart*, and *Aftermath: Picking Up the Pieces After a Suicide*. Gary's books have won four international book awards and have been named finalists seven times. He has been featured on Dr. Laura, Belief Net, the Christian Broadcasting Network, Wellness, Thrive Global, and other major media and has well over 800 grief-related articles in print. Recipient of the Diane Duncam Award for Excellence in Hospice Care, Gary is a popular keynote, conference, and seminar speaker at a wide variety of venues.

Gary loves being a husband and father. He has seven adopted children, including three daughters from Colombia. He enjoys hockey, corny jokes, good puns, and colorful Hawaiian shirts. Gary and his wife Jen and family live in Texas.

**Visit Gary at www.garyroe.com.**

**Download your exclusive, free, printable PDF:
Scriptures and Prayers from *Widowed Walk*
www.garyroe.com/grief-prayers**

# Acknowledgments

Special thanks for my lovely wife Jen for her constant and unwavering support and encouragement. Thank you for engaging with me in giving hope and bringing healing.

Special thanks to Kathy Trim and Kelli Levey Reynolds for their keen proofreading eyes and editorial assistance. I appreciate you more than you know.

Thanks to Dr. Craig Borchardt of Hospice Brazos Valley for his continued support in producing quality resources for grieving hearts. It's an honor to work under your supervision.

Thanks to Glendon Haddix of Streetlight Graphics for his artistic skill and expertise in design and formatting. Your artistry continues to bring healing and hope to many.

# An Urgent Plea

## HELP OTHER GRIEVING HEARTS

Dear Reader,

Others are hurting and grieving today. You can help. How?

With a simple, heartfelt review.

Could you take a few moments and write a 1-3 sentence review of *Widowed Walk* and leave it on the site you purchased the book from?

And if you want to help even more, you could leave the same review on the *Widowed Walk* book page on Goodreads.

Your review counts and will help reach others who could benefit from this book.

Thanks for considering this. I read these reviews as well, and your comments and feedback assist me in producing more quality resources for grieving hearts.

Thank you!
Warmly,
Gary